NEWS MEDIA VERSE
The Agnew Probe

Kenneth Vailes

MINERVA PRESS
MONTREUX LONDON WASHINGTON

NEWS MEDIA VERSE: *The Agnew Probe*
Copyright © Kenneth Vailes 1999

All Rights Reserved

No part of this book may be reproduced in any form
by photocopying or by any electronic or mechanical means,
including information storage or retrieval systems,
without permission in writing from both the copyright
owner and the publisher of this book.

ISBN 1 85863 681 7

First Published 1999 by
MINERVA PRESS
315–317 Regent Street
London W1R 7YB

Printed in Great Britain for Minerva Press

NEWS MEDIA VERSE
The Agnew Probe

Contents

Introduction	xi
The Agnew Probe	13
Figures linked to Maryland probe	15
They'll sink or swim together	21
Agnew's response refreshing	23
Agnew adopting independent role	26
Contractors sought favors 4 say Agnew got money	27
Support for Agnew jams Western Union	29
Nixon keeps distance from Agnew	30
Laird's warning about Agnew	32
Straw men for Agnew	35
Two-thirds in poll back Agnew so far	38
The Vice-Presidency	40
Agnew lent support to friend's firm	44
Kerner, Agnew and Justice	46
Richardson decides to allow probe	49

Agnew departure said discussed	52
Funneling of cash to Agnew reported	54
Bearing down on the high court…	56
Mr. Agnew: a stone wall at justice	59
The Agnew case: Mr. Nixon's options	62
Request for probe rejected by Albert Evidence set for U.S. jury today	65
Won't act on Agnew note to hill	67
'Toughing it out' for three more years	69
Law, order and rights	72
Agnew declares he won't resign even if indicted	75
Agnew's assault	77
Mr. Agnew's California speech	79
Agnew's plight	82
Agnew: 'hanged without a trial'	85
Nixon calls Agnew move 'proper' one	88
The impeachment – first approach	90
Agnew to keep speaking out Taking 'Case to the Country'	93
Agnew to fight validity of probe	94
Agnew's letter	96

The amazing, gutsy Richardson	98
Mr. Agnew and the Vice Presidency	100
Goldwater's warning	104
Agnew: the President's comment	105
A vindication scenario for Agnew	107
A bitter family dispute	110
Petersen and the leaks	113
The Press and the Agnew case	116
Four friends from the old days	121
New challenge to press freedom	126
A subdued Agnew praises President	129
Offers house time to act Agnew not immune, justice dept. insists	131
Jury probes Agnew home purchase	133
With Agnew, duty first	136
The fate of other vice-presidents under fire	139
Pleads on tax evasion Agnew resigns	142
Agnew decision 'stunned' staff	144
Agnew big news around the world	146
'The man is a crook,' U.S. Attorney says	148
'And then they knifed him' Agnew resignation evokes some bitter views	149

Agnew departure jolts Marylanders	152
Anonymous call to IRS office sparked Agnew investigation	157
Resignation draws a mixed reaction	160
Press suit by Agnew held moot	163
'A good deal for everyone'	165
Pat Nixon 'saddened'	168
Yet Agnew did what needed doing	169
By God, it hurts	172
Agnew's 'no contest' plea may prompt move by IRS	175
Agnew seen retaining civil rights but the IRS and Maryland are expected to file tax actions	177
'He resigned because he had no choice'	181
District takes news with cynicism, gloom	184
Three months short resignation cost pension	187
All due reverent speed	188
Mr. Agnew's resignation	191
Choosing the new Vice President	195
Paying attention to Watergate	198
Ford got 90-minute notice 'The President is Calling'	201
The choice of Mr. Ford	203

Loyalty is rewarded	206
Explaining away Agnew's tragedy	209
Agnew, the truth and a free press	212
List of Contributors	215

Introduction

What you are about to read is a series of editorial comments, and a selection of newspaper articles by the news media.

These news articles were published in the *Star News* and the *Washington Post* during the Seventies.

These journalist of distinction wrote to tell a story. The story is about Vice-President Spiro T. Agnew. He was forced to resign the office of Vice-President of the United State of America in disgrace.

When these journalist wrote about Spiro T. Agnew they also wrote about President Richard Nixon and the Watergate scandal. These two men, Vice-President Spiro T. Agnew and President Richard Nixon were under investigation on completely different charges.

The news media is not perfect but these journalists do an excellent job of writing about world affairs.

One of the journalist spoke to say, 'the issue has been clear-cut through the centuries since Plato's warning to public men, "Do no service for a present".'

Kenneth Vailes

The Agnew Probe

Well, as they say, it never rains but it pours. It was one of the consolations of these recent unhappy months that at least one person in the Executive Office Building, Vice-President Spiro T. Agnew, was untainted by the Watergate mess. Now comes the word that Agnew has been formally notified by US Attorney George Beall (brother of Republican Senator J. Glenn Beall) that he is under criminal investigation in connection with alleged kickbacks paid to government officials by building contractors, architects and engineers.

It should be stated immediately that the Vice-President has not been formally indicted or accused of any crime, and he may not be. It is reported that the testimony against Agnew and two associates has come from persons who are themselves targets of the investigation and their testimony may be discredited at a future date. The Vice-President has protested his innocence, and it would be both unfair and unwise to make any assumptions about his involvement in Baltimore County shenanigans while he was county executive (1962–66), Governor (1966–68) or Vice-President.

Indeed, this is not the first time that the suggestion has been made that Agnew was involved in wrongdoing while he held state office. Yet there has never been a scintilla of proof offered to substantiate these allegations.

Nevertheless, coming as it does against the bitter divisiveness of the Watergate scandal, the fact that allegations of bribery and tax fraud have been made against the Vice-President is a stunning blow. That the letter telling Agnew he was a target of the probe was cleared through Attorney General Elliot L. Richardson, who has informed Special Watergate prosecutor Archibald Cox, would seem to indicate that the gravity of the situation was fully understood by Beall's office.

Should Agnew be invited or subpoenaed to testify before a Grand Jury, the same question of the separation of powers which President Nixon has invoked in the Watergate case may arise. It is not clear, for instance, if a President or a Vice-President can be indicated without first being impeached.

We earnestly hope that the question will not arise, and that the allegations against the Vice-President will be found to be groundless. What the country does not need at this time is the unprecedented situation under which both the President and the Vice-President, perhaps equally unfairly are under suspicion of wrongdoing. Our institutions are both strong and resilient, but they can only be subjected to so much strain before, as Supreme Court Justice Harry A. Blackmun put it the other day, the 'very glue of our ship of state' becomes unstuck.

For this reason if for no other, let there be no rush to judgment.

Editorial Comment
The *Star News*

Figures linked to Maryland probe

Jerome Benjamin Wolff moved from Towson to Annapolis to Washington as his political patron, Spiro T. Agnew, rose from Baltimore County executive to the governorship of Maryland and then to the Vice-Presidency.

As the county's Assistant Director of Public Works and later as the Vice-Presidential Assistant for Science and Technology, 'Jerry' Wolff worked in the background.

But in state government, where he served as Chairman-Director of the old State Roads Commission from 1967 to 1969, Wolff was perhaps the most visible, voluble, outspoken and energetic member of Agnew's administrative team.

Early in the Agnew administration, when the new governor was taking a roadshow of top officials on a get-acquainted tour of county courthouses, Wolff mastered the art of delivering bad news with witty one-lines that would dissolve his disappointed audiences into laughter.

He would frequently entertain fellow members of the roads commission, who were chosen as a reward for past political services, by commenting on some development with an apt quotation from Shakespeare or another classic author.

Sometimes he would interrupt meetings, take off his horn-rimmed glasses and tell a joke.

His tenure at the Roads Commission – which has since been reorganized and made part of the State Department of Transportation – is still remembered as the time when tradition became second to performance.

'He didn't care that this is the way we've always done something,' a former associate recalled yesterday. 'If a new way is better, he'd say 'let's change'. We did.'

A Chicago-born lawyer and engineer specializing in environmental matters, Wolff moved to Maryland in 1952 and served in various Baltimore County positions before becoming the No. 2 man in the Public Works Department.

When tapped by Agnew for the roads post, Wolff agreed to divest himself of all interest in his two engineering consulting firms. Agnew said at the time that the terms of his appointment 'go considerably beyond the requirements of the conflict-of-interest law'.

Since leaving the Vice-Presidential staff in 1970, Wolff became President of Greiner Environmental Systems, Inc., an affiliate of a major Baltimore firm that has done much work for the state government, including consulting for the recently-completed parallel Chesapeake Bay Bridge.

Now 55, he lives with his wife in Stevenson, a northwest suburb of Baltimore. He has two grown stepchildren.

Wolff is reported to be one target of the Federal Grand Jury in Baltimore investigating possible violations of bribery, conspiracy and tax laws in connection with an alleged kickback scheme. He and Lester Matz, another target of the investigation, have been hinting to investigators, according to sources, that in return for immunity or reduced charges they would be willing to supply information about Agnew.

William Fornoff

Until he resigned and pleaded guilty to a relatively minor tax law violation in early June, William E. Fornoff was in charge of managing Baltimore County's government – a $238-million-a-year operation.

Tall, stocky, gray-haired and noted as a good dresser, Fornoff, 56, had been outspoken in his dealings with the Baltimore County Council, before which he was the chief representative of the county administration. Some Council members referred to him as 'Wild Bill'.

The county he worked for, which almost surrounds the city of Baltimore, is Maryland's second largest in population (its 630,000 total is second only to Prince George's County). It includes both Maryland's heaviest industry – the Sparrow's Point steel complex – and its most fashionable society – among the residents of the Green Spring Valley hunt country north of the city.

Fornoff had held the job since 1957, except for a 15-month period in 1965–66 when he worked for the Arundel Corp., a sand and gravel company.

He was the No. 2 county official and served under four elected county executives, including Spiro T. Agnew (1962–66) and Dale Anderson, the democrat who succeeded Agnew.

A resident of Lutherville near the county seat in Towson, Fornoff is said to love hunting pheasant on Maryland's Eastern Shore.

Fornoff's office was on the third floor of the County Office Building next to the County Executive's and a large conference room. One county official recalled yesterday that Fornoff 'sat there (in the conference room) like Henry VIII calling in the underlings and laying down the law'.

On June 4, Fornoff pleaded guilty to one count of interfering with the administration of Federal internal revenue laws, a felony with a maximum sentence of three years in jail and a $5,000 fine. He has not yet been sentenced.

Before entering his plea, Fornoff told a Federal Grand Jury in Baltimore that since 1967 he had funneled cash kickbacks from several local contractors 'to another official in Baltimore County'.

I.H. Hammerman

I.H. (Bud) Hammerman is one of the leading financial and civic leaders in Baltimore, a busy and energetic man whose home base is his family's mortgage banking business.

'He covers a million things and goes everywhere, and I don't know how he does it,' says the Executive Director of the Advertising Club of Baltimore, of which Hammerman is a board member and past President.

The family business, the S.L. Hammerman Organization, Inc., was begun by his father, the late Sam Hammerman, who began his career as a bricklayer and saved enough money by living frugally to buy land and start building apartments.

Young Hammerman, a graduate of the Wharton School of Finance and Commerce and the University of Pennsylvania, joined his father's firm after serving in the Military in World War II.

'Mr "Sam" made his son "work" his way up rather than being stuck in there as an officer right off the bat,' according to a friend, Howard Scaggs, President of American National Building and Loan Association. His first job was as a construction worker.

Hammerman followed his father's example not only in the business world but in civic and philanthropic activities. He has served on the board of directors of Loyola College of Baltimore (to which his father donated the library) and the University of Pennsylvania, and has been an officer of the Chamber of Commerce and other organizations. Friends say he has donated generously to schools, synagogues, churches and charities.

In the middle 1960s Sam Hammerman died and his son took over the Presidency of the mortgage banking business, which also owns and manages apartment and office buildings.

Hammerman, who lives with his wife and four children in the fashionable Upper-Park Heights section of Baltimore, is described by friends and associates as 'very aggressive and dynamic', 'very congenial' and 'very patriotic.'

He is described as a longtime and close friend of Vice-President Agnew, and served as campaign chairman when Agnew ran successfully for Governor in 1966.

Lester Matz

Matz is one of those under investigation by the Federal Grand Jury in Baltimore and, according to sources, is one of two persons (the other is Jerome B. Wolff) who have been hinting to investigators that in return for immunity or reduced charges they would be willing to supply information on Agnew.

J. Walter Jones

J. Walter Jones is described by a Baltimore political figure as being, along with I.H. (Bud) Hammerman, 'very close to Agnew – the comparison would be with the guys around the President – Bebe Rebozo and Robert Abplanalp'.

Jones, a wealthy Annapolis banker and real estate man, has been a principal fund-raiser for Maryland Republicans, and particularly Agnew.

Now he, Agnew and Hammerman are reported to be under Federal investigation for possible violation of bribery, conspiracy and tax laws.

Editorial Staff
The *Star News*

They'll sink or swim together

Spiro Agnew's troubles impart a double-or-nothing character to the outcome of Watergate. For if the Vice-President survives, he will provide almost iron-clad insurance against pressures to force President Nixon from office.

But if Mr Agnew is found seriously culpable, Mr Nixon's troubles will be greatly intensified. There will be set in motion a procedure apt to end in the ouster of both men.

To grasp the situation, it is first necessary to get a feel for the pace of the inquiry into the allegations against the Vice-President. Contrary to widespread impression, the investigation into Mr Agnew's case is still at an early stage. Witnesses have not yet been sworn and records have not yet been fully examined. Something like a month will probably have to go by before there is a determination one way or another in the case of the Vice-President.

Already, however, it is clear that the case against Mr Agnew is grave. From the US Attorney, George Beall, to the Attorney General Elliot Richardson. Those responsible for the prosecution are serious men, well known for support of the Nixon administration and with no axes to grind against the Vice-President. Yet they felt the allegations against Mr Agnew warranted a formal notification and a very tough letter requesting extensive personal records.

Moreover, the response by the rest of the administration has hardly been reassuring. The President has not come personally to the defense of his Vice-President. Mr Agnew's first response – an affirmation of faith in the system of criminal justice – read like the confession of a man who hoped to get off easy. His second response – the press conference of last week – was tough in manner but very cagey on points of law. For example, Mr Agnew asked for time to consider whether executive privilege might forbid his handing over documents to the prosecution. But if the charges really were 'damned lies,' as he said, his interest would be to waive the privilege at once in order to surface the records that prove his innocence.

Finally, Maryland, like New Jersey and Illinois, is one of those states where the political tradition is dirty. As a county executive and Governor, Mr Agnew played the game, to put it mildly.

The most Mr Agnew can hope for accordingly, is to avoid indictment, because of lack of proof. Even in that case some sleazy associates and dubious past practices are bound to become widely known. At best, in other words, the Vice-President will emerge bloodied and bowed.

But a tarnished Agnew still in place is Mr Nixon's best possible defense against Watergate. For if it becomes clear that forcing Mr Nixon out meant bringing Mr Agnew into the White House, almost everybody, and especially the Democrats, would draw back from pressing Watergate to the hilt against the President.

Joseph Kraft

Agnew's response refreshing

What this town has been hoping for recently is somebody, anybody in power, who would stand up and give plain answers to hard questions, and Vice-President Agnew has finally done it.

When the Justice Department informed him officially that he was being 'investigated for using his influence and taking bribes on government contracts', he didn't duck for long behind legal barriers, but called a press conference and said it was a 'damned lie'.

He didn't hide for weeks or months behind 'executive privilege' or issue proclamations about his 'legal rights'. After a short but unfortunate delay, he saw the reality. The headlines in the newspapers made him look like a crook, so he came out fighting.

The courts will decide later whether there was any wrongdoing in this case. The only point here now is how a public official should react when there is even a suspicion of wrongdoing, and Agnew demonstrated how to do it.

He didn't ask, but told the President he was going to call a press conference at three o'clock the next afternoon. He didn't have a few 'friends' in the press around to hear his story, but invited everybody, TV cameras and all. He asked for the tough questions, and he got them.

Had he ever taken any money from government contractors? No! Was there a problem about politicians and government contractors? Sure, he said, you would be 'naive' if you didn't recognize it. Had he ever been offered a bribe to use his influence in public office? Yes, once when he was too inexperienced to know what was happening, but it had nothing to do with this case. Had he thought of resigning or standing down while these charges were going through the courts? Certainly not, he didn't believe he would be indicted.

He was cautious about committing himself to appear before a Grand Jury or about handing over personal papers to the courts, not for personal reasons, but because this obviously raised constitutional questions that also touch on President Nixon's problems in the Watergate case, but he insisted that he had nothing to hide, would make all relevant documents available at the appropriate time, and, while listening to legal counsel, would decide on his own what to do.

The contrast with President Nixon, who hasn't had a press conference during the Watergate crisis since March 15, was unavoidable. So maybe something important is happening here.

Even at the top of the Nixon administration, officials are beginning to speak out. The new Attorney General, Elliot Richardson, didn't ask whether the Agnew 'investigation' would embarrass the President or the Vice-President, but simply advised Agnew that he was being investigated for possible criminal action.

This is a change worth noting. It is not only the Ervin Committee and other members of Congress who are beginning to show a new independence, but also key members of the President's own executive family.

Vice-President Agnew's press conference is only one important symbol.

And the reaction to this was startling. For even without knowing the facts in Agnew's case, the feeling after his press conference was very much in his favor in fact, that finally in this town somebody in power had talked up with candor and passion, and taken the risk of telling the truth.

James Reston

Agnew adopting independent role

Richard Nixon once called the Vice-Presidency 'a holiday shell – the most ill-conceived, poorly defined position in the American political system'.

This is an accurate description of Spiro Theodore Agnew's role as it has evolved under Mr Nixon's own Presidency.

Until it was revealed last week that Agnew was under investigation for purportedly accepting kickbacks from Maryland contractors, the Vice-President had been steadily fading back into the household obscurity from which Mr Nixon had rescued him in 1968.

But Agnew's practice of playing second violin in the White House orchestra ended last week on an abrupt discordant note. After a 1¾-hour meeting with Mr Nixon described by White House sources as 'acrimonious', Agnew emerged firmly committed to an outspoken course of action that he knows may be contrasted to President Nixon's policy of silence and half-statements about Watergate.

In the new atmosphere of independence, Agnew aides and supporters now tell a story of repeated humiliations by the White House; telephone calls which H.R. Haldeman never bothered to return; domestic decisions which Agnew was 'frozen out of' by John Ehrlichman; carefully arranged White House news leaks that undercut Agnew while he was abroad.

Lou Cannon

Contractors sought favors 4 say Agnew got money

At least four Baltimore County contractors have told Federal prosecutors that they made 'cash payments' to Vice-President Spiro T. Agnew in hopes of getting favored treatment in the awarding of government consulting contracts, according to reliable sources.

It is not known where the contractors are claiming that they actually received special consideration in the awarding of contracts, most of which are given on a non-competitive basis. Nor is it clear whether they are saying that the alleged payments were in the form of contributions to Agnew's political campaigns.

The four businessmen are offering to trade testimony about the alleged 'payments' in return for immunity from prosecution, sources said. It was not known whether the contractors claim that they have documentary evidence to support their charges.

One highly placed source said yesterday that the prosecutors in the case feel that 'there is a long way to go between the claiming, the proving and showing that the money was received'.

Agnew has declared that he is innocent of any misconduct and has denounced charges against him as 'damned lies'.

It was learned yesterday that evidence concerning Agnew will be presented to a special Grand Jury in Baltimore beginning late this week or early next week.

Two of the four contractors who are bargaining with Federal officials were identified by sources as Lester Matz, a partner in the Baltimore consulting engineering firm of Matz, Childs and Associates and Jerome B. Wolff, President of Greiner Environmental Systems, Inc., a subsidiary of the J.E. Greiner Co., another engineering consulting firm.

The identities of the other two consultants was not immediately known.

Matz and Wolff have been under investigation by the US Attorney's Office in Baltimore and the special Grand Jury for possible involvement in payoffs by contractors to government officials in Maryland.

Both the Matz, Childs and Greiner firms won numerous contracts with the state during the time Agnew was Governor.

Matz, Childs has worked on the widening of the John F. Kennedy Memorial Highway and construction of approaches to the Baltimore Harbor Tunnel.

The J.E. Greiner Co. was the consulting engineering firm for the new $118 million Chesapeake Bay Bridge.

Agnew was named as a target in the probe earlier this month in a letter to one of his lawyers from US Attorney George Beall. The Vice-President was notified that he is under investigation for bribery, extortion, conspiracy and income tax violations.

Jerry Oppenheimer,
Robert Walters

Support for Agnew jams Western Union

Hundreds of telegrams supporting Vice-President Agnew have poured into the Western Union Office here.

One Western Union employee said there were 'a mountain of telegrams. It's just like President Nixon's China trip'.

Miss Clarie Williams, the night supervisor at the Western Union's local office, said more than 300 telegrams addressed to Agnew arrived after his televised news conference. But Mrs Williams said they were primarily the overflow.

'Most of them are fed into the computer which sends them direct to the Senate,' where Agnew has his constitutional office. Miss Williams said, 'we never see those here'.

Miss Williams said the volume was heavy, but that it was 'nowhere near' what the President receives after some of his televised speeches.

United Press International

Nixon keeps distance from Agnew

President Nixon is withholding from embattled Vice-President Spiro T. Agnew a public declaration of 'you're my boy'.

White House aides insist privately that Nixon is giving Agnew his full support. But the Vice-President said yesterday he has no expectation that Nixon will extend him a public endorsement any time soon.

Agnew informed Nixon in early May that he was under investigation by the US Attorney's Office in Baltimore for possible violations of the bribery, extortion, conspiracy and tax laws.

But aides said it still shocked the White House when Agnew reported last week that he had received a formal letter from US Atty. George Beall telling him of his rights under the 5th Amendment and soliciting his voluntary co-operation.

Agnew's current position parallels in some respects the predicament Nixon faced almost 21 years ago when his privately raised political fund was revealed. Nixon, then a candidate for Vice-President, responded with his now famous 'Checkers' speech in which he gave his side of the story.

In his autobiography, Six Crises, Nixon said he was so angered by what he considered a lukewarm endorsement from the presidential candidate, Gen. Dwight D.

Eisenhower, that he drafted a letter resigning from the ticket.

But Nixon remained the candidate after Eisenhower summoned his to a face to face meeting in Wheeling, W. Va., where he greeted him with, 'You're my boy'.

Agnew told a news conference that Nixon 'did express confidence in me, directly to me,' during a meeting Tuesday afternoon in the President's office. Nixon and Agnew were alone for almost two hours. The meeting was not announced until yesterday.

But Nixon has made no public gesture. He has not been photographed with Agnew recently and he has said nothing publicly of the Vice-President's legal problems either verbally or in writing.

Deputy press secretary Gerald L. Warren said the White House would do nothing to 'interfere with or prejudge the investigation' by Beall.

Warren then offered a description of Nixon's attitude toward Agnew that sounded like very faint praise. But White House aides insisted later that Warren had intended to indicate that Nixon retains full confidence in his Vice-President.

'The fact that there is this investigation pending in Maryland is no reason for the President to change attitude about the Vice-President or his confidence in the Vice-President,' Warren said.

Norman Kempster

Laird's warning about Agnew

A confidential telephone call from top White House aide Melvin R. Laird to a Republican congressional leader, warning him not to go all-out in defense of Vice-President Spiro Agnew, is new and hard evidence to party professionals of the depth of the crisis that threatens Mr Agnew.

In his Aug. 7 telephone call to Rep. John B. Anderson of Illinois, Chairman of the House Republican Conference, Laird carefully specified that he was not talking as a White House aide. His message: Don't get on a limb in the Agnew affair, particularly with an all out defense of the Vice-President. Stay away from the Agnew affair as far as possible.

Agnew is under intense Federal investigation on charges of possible criminal violations of various Federal statutes involving bribery, extortion, tax fraud and conspiracy.

Republicans who know about the Laird call to Anderson, described as 'astonished' by the warning, assume that Laird and possible other party grandees have contacted other senior Republicans with similar warnings.

Moreover, the Laird telephone call to Anderson fits a pattern that has infuriated the Agnew camp. For example:

1. Before Agnew himself received formal notice from the Justice Department that he was under investigation, Attorney General Elliot Richardson reported (in late July) to White House staff chief Alexander M. Haig Jr.,

with a briefing on all aspects of the case. On Aug. 2. Agnew's attorneys received their letter from the prosecutors.

2. A prominent television commentator was privately cautioned by an official of the Justice Department 10 days ago in words similar to those used by Laird to Anderson. Don't go overboard for Agnew: you may wind up with egg on your face.
3. The White House has gone to embarrassing lengths not to put the President on record as to the Vice-President's innocence. White House spokesman Gerald Warren will only say that Mr Nixon's confidence in Agnew has not changed.
4. The *New York Times* front-page dispatch of Aug. 15 outlining charges against Agnew in vivid detail, is believed by furious Agnew allies to have emanated from high levels of the Justice Department (who flatly deny it), not from Maryland sources also implicated in the charges against Agnew.

It is not surprising that allies of Agnew, whose talents have sometimes been grossly used by the President to advance Mr Nixon's interests would be filled with dark suspicion over these incidents. They regard them as proof of nefarious underground administration warfare against Agnew, partly to ease the President's immense Watergate burdens. Thus, in this conspiratorial view – so understandable on the part of Agnew intimates – Mr Nixon or Republicans close to him are greasing the skids for the hapless Vice-President. Under the 25th amendment to the Constitution, they are quietly preparing to nominate a successor – most likely John B. Connally.

It was Connally who saved Mr Nixon from disaster in the inflationary crisis of August 1971. Perhaps Connally, the former Democratic Governor of Texas who turned Republican at a moment of maximum help to the Watergate-beleaguered President last spring, can help again. To Agnewites, that fits the known fact that Connally recently canceled his plans for a long trip abroad and the lesser-known fact that some Connally friends predict he will be back in the administration in October.

But, in fact, the Laird warnings may spring from something far less conspiratorial. They may be a flashing signal of caution based not on any desire to do in Agnew but on a rational and informed judgment that Agnew is a goner. Likewise, Richardson's July briefing of Haig, before Agnew himself had formal notification, may also be explainable as a rational act based on the President's prior right to know. 'Is that normal?' a Justice Department official repeated in answer to our question. 'Hell, nothing's normal in this case. We're playing it by ear.'

But such quiet and rational explanation is understandably difficult for Agnewites. The mood in the Agnew camp has grown isolated and embittered. Now, with word secretly passed to 'keep clear' of the Agnew affair, that mood will intensify, with dangerous implications for the Republican future no matter how the investigation finally ends.

Rowland Evans,
Robert Novak

Straw men for Agnew

Vice-President Agnew appeared to be at his alliterative apogee the other night when he told a Republican audience that 'we have reached the watershed of Watergate' (although that could be taken to mean that everything will be downhill from here on). When he got to his main theme, however, Agnew sounded like nothing so much as a nattering nabob of Nixonism.

Watergate, he said, was 'the misguided actions of a few zealots' that had been blown into a storm by the 'rain dance' of Sen. Ervin and his committee. The true story was that 'embittered critics of this administration and the Republican) party who could not discredit us at the polls in November will make every effort – no matter how reckless – to discredit us now.'

Well, there are some 'embittered critics' on this administration all right, but no one other than Agnew has suggested that the Republican party was to be blamed for Watergate; and in fact, no one other than Agnew has suggested that the Republican party was even involved in the Nixon re-election effort, since he neither used its name and machinery nor campaigned for its other candidates.

Apart from all that, and bearing in mind Agnew's useful reminder that those accused have not necessarily been proven guilty of anything, it is undeniable fact that:

1. Seven former employees of the Nixon White House, the Nixon re-election committee, or both, have been convicted of crimes.
2. Four former Nixon White House staff members have been indicted as a result of the burglary of a psychiatrist's office in Los Angeles in 1971.
3. Although no other Cabinet or former Cabinet official has been indicated for criminal acts for nearly half a century, two former Nixon Cabinet officers, who also were at one time the highest ranking officers of his re-election committee, went on trial this week for obstruction of justice, conspiracy and perjury.
4. These cases resulted not from rain-dancing in the Senate but from the deliberations of three separate grand juries in Los Angeles, Washington and New York.
5. At least a dozen officials of the Nixon administration have resigned or been fired in connection with the Watergate and related scandals, all within less than three months.
6. At least one major company has admitted making an illegal contribution the Nixon re-election committee, under pressure from its fund-raisers and with an eye to a case pending before a government regulatory agency.

Without prejudging any of these facts as to the guilt or innocence of any person charged, this record alone is more than enough to refute the Agnevian asininity that 'embittered critics' are merely doing through Watergate what they could not do at the polls. Who could even have conceived such a conspiracy, let alone carried it through?

In fact, Agnew – himself potentially in trouble because of an investigation that might reach still a fourth Grand Jury in still a fourth city P appeared mostly to be reaching mostly for needed political support within his party and within the White House, in both of which he undoubtedly needs it.

The President and his lawyers may well have a good deal to say – if not the final say – as to whether the Agnew case goes to Grand Jury; if Agnew is indicted, the President could and probably would bring tremendous pressure on him to resign, so that Nixon could nominate a new man. Agnew had good reason, therefore, to parrot the White House line that its enemies are out to get Nixon.

He had good reason, too, to make a valiant defense of a Republican party that is not noticeably under attack.

The same night he spoke, John B. Connally Jr., Sam Yorty's predecessor in party-switching was appearing before an important California Republican assembly the next day, that states Gov. Ronald Reagan plugged his tricky new tax plan before the same group. Republicans being notably clannish, Connally apparently got an apostate's welcome, Reagan one for a hero. But each is a potential heir to Agnew's hitherto solid conservative backing at a time when every indicator suggests the investigation hanging over his head already has dimmed the Vice-President's prospects for 1976.

Not that Nixon would necessarily choose one of these two for Vice-President if Agnew had to resign. Unless the President has changed his mind in recent years, he would rule out Reagan because of the Governor's know-nothingism in foreign affairs; and to give a recently recycled Democrat like Connally such an important political leg-up might well split the Republican party for 1976 and further alienate congressional Democrats.

But with so many – the Grand Jury, Nixon, Connally, Reagan – breathing hotly on his neck, Agnew can hardly be blamed for setting up 'embittered critics' as straw men he could knock over. That's just good Nixonism.

Tom Wicker

Two-thirds in poll back Agnew so far

New York (UPI) – Two-thirds of the American public are opposed to Vice-President Agnew resigning now, but fifty-eight percent would approve his leaving office if he is indicted, a *Newsweek*-Gallup poll reported yesterday.

The findings, scheduled to appear in the magazine's Oct. 1 issue, also disclosed an 'undercurrent of suspicion' that President Nixon may not be treating Agnew fairly, *Newsweek* said. Only forty percent agree that Nixon is being fair to the Vice-President, while thirty-five percent says he is not, and twenty-five percent voiced no opinion.

The findings were the result of a *Newsweek*-sponsored telephone survey of a 631-person cross section of Americans conducted by the Gallup organization late last week.

Asked if they thought the Vice-President should resign if he is indicted, fifty-eight percent said he should, thirty percent said he should not and twelve percent had no opinion. Only sixteen percent thought Agnew should resign now, while sixty-six percent said he should not.

Former Secretary of Treasury John Connally, with twenty-four percentage points headed the list of six potential candidates to succeed Agnew if he resigned, followed by Sen. Barry Goldwater, R-Ariz., with nineteen percent, and Sen. Howard Baker, R-Tenn., fifteen percent.

The others included New York's Gov. Nelson Rockefeller, fourteen percent; Atty. Gen. Elliot Richardson, five percent, and former Secretary of State William Rogers, four percent.

Newsweek said an unusually large number – eighty-nine percent – of those polled said they were familiar with the investigation of Agnew.

United Press International

The Vice-Presidency

It is a measure of the strangeness of the times that so many things once deemed exotic or unthinkable have become the common currency of public talk. One subject in this category is the possibility that Vice-President Agnew might resign. Speculation has been fueled by the skeptical, not to say cynical, atmosphere which now prevails, and by the absence of hard facts, either about Mr. Agnew's own state of mind, or about the views and pressures being exerted at the White House or, most important, about the precise nature of the allegations involving the Vice-President which are now under investigation in Baltimore.

Given all of those unknowns, a judgment on whether Mr Agnew should resign is both premature and unjustifiable. And yet the issue is upon us if only because the possibility is being fiercely debated in public as well as in private. Like it or not, an unprecedented event – the possibility of having to replace a Vice-President in mid-term – has emerged as a contingency which, however remote, deserves serious contemplation.

Under normal circumstances, the selection of Vice-Presidential candidates is the most haphazard and arbitrary process in American politics – and yet one of the most portentous. Vice-Presidential nominees often turn out to be more than just running mates. Three of our last five Presidents have come to the office via the Vice-Presidency, either on the death of the incumbent President or through nomination and election to the Presidency after having been elevated to public prominence by service in the second post. One-third of all American Presidents had prior service as Vice-President. Yet, in the usual course of events – the frenzy and sleeplessness of national political conventions – Vice-Presidential candidates are chosen in the worst of ways, usually at the whim or calculation of a presidential nominee, often in response to transient political demands, and sometimes with all too little knowledge of a candidate's background and fitness for the job. Under the extraordinary circumstances of a mid-term vacancy, the process would be governed by the 25th Amendment, but that is a skeleton clause which has not been fleshed out by law or precedent. It provides:

> Whenever there is a vacancy in the office of the Vice-President, the President shall nominate a Vice-President who shall take office upon confirmation by a majority of both Houses of Congress.

Since this amendment was ratified only six years ago and has never been used, President Nixon – if required to make such a nomination – would be acting in a formless field without the guidance which history and tradition can provide. Yet the President's choice, and the manner of choosing, could have a powerful impact on American politics and the future course of the country for years to come. To begin with, a sitting President would be selecting his own replacement in the event he were unable to complete his present term. Beyond that, he might well be selecting his successor, or at least a future President, given the record of past Vice-Presidents for moving on to the Presidency. It is axiomatic that any potential Republican Presidential candidate so favored by Mr Nixon under these circumstances would have a tremendous advantage in the contest for the nomination in 1976. But the singling out of such a candidate, particularly a controversial figure, with little advance consultation and with only perfunctory Congressional deliberation. In an atmosphere of 'national emergency', could further disillusion and embitter a public afflicted by a sense that government is already far too removed, unresponsive and irresponsible. This, in itself, would argue strongly for the selection of an elder statesman without Presidential ambitions or of a unifying figure named only after frank and extensive consultation with many party leaders.

Much could depend, in other words, on such political factors as which phone calls Mr Nixon decided to make, and to take, before setting on a nominee, and on the attitude and pace with which he approaches the problem of arriving at his choice. Much could also turn on how the Congress – especially a Congress controlled by the opposition party – handled the nomination. The sobering fact is that the Congress, which has procedures for almost everything else, has no rules at all for considering a Vice-Presidential nomination. How should the qualifications of a nominee – his fitness to assume the Presidency – be evaluated? Who should interrogate the nominee? Should a special committee be created in each house? How long should floor debate proceed? Such elementary procedural matters will no doubt have to be settled at some point, either by the 93rd Congress or a future one.

The course of prudence and responsibility would be to begin working out these matters now, so that whenever any President and any Congress have to deal with the first mid-term Vice-Presidential vacancy, the ground rules will already have been set. A failure to anticipate such contingencies and to weigh alternatives candidly can only compound the likelihood of political mischief, emotionalism and arbitrary acts at what could be a critical juncture in our national life. At the very least, if the Vice-

Presidential contingency now before us should become a reality, the public and the Congress would deserve something better than a summary decision handed down in a way which forecloses the freest possible play of the political process.

Editorial Comment
The *Star News*

Agnew lent support to friend's firm

Vice-President Spiro Agnew has twice pressured a small Federal agency and to give handsome no-bid contracts to a Maryland company run by an old friend and political campaign contributor.

The lucky company was Maps Inc., of Baltimore, which does aerial photography and related mapping. Until his death in January, 1971, its President was Thomas Collins, who had been a member of the Baltimore County Personnel and Salary Board while Agnew was the county's Chief Executive.

A few months after Agnew became Vice-President, Collins began to seek a $121,900 air map contract with the Redevelopment Land Agency, a housing and planning agency in Washington. Aware of his old friend's new power in Washington, Collins called Agnew.

Agnew had an aide call RLA, and the agency awarded the contract to Maps Inc. One competitor protested loudly to RLA that political pressure had been exerted, but the complaint was ignored.

In 1971, RLA was preparing to award another mapping contract, and the agency's Executive Director, Melvin Mister, got an unusual letter from Agnew's administrative assistant, Arthur Sohmer.

'Two years ago,' Sohmer reminded Mister, 'this office contacted you on behalf of Maps Inc., a Baltimore firm, which had expressed an interest in doing topographic mapping for your agency.'

The Vice-Presidential message went on to praise Maps inc., at some length, then added pointedly: 'Any consideration that you might be able to give to their interest would be appreciated by this office.'

On Sept. 24, exactly a month after the Agnew letter, Maps Inc., got a $158,600 contract from RLA. Once again, a competing firm told RLA it had been unfairly treated.

In Dundalk, Md. the Baltimore suburb where Maps Inc., is located, Mrs Collins, who briefly succeeded her husband as President, explained: 'The Agnews were our friends. Tom and Ted knew each other well. So did Judy (Agnew's wife) and I. They lived about a mile from us.'

She insisted that to the best of her knowledge her late husband's political donations to Agnew were in the form of fund-raising tickets and were at most in the low hundreds.

At RLA, a spokesman said Maps Inc., 'did a good job on both contracts' – which our study of the files tends to confirm. The spokesman said: 'It was a validly awarded contract. The contacts (by Agnew's office) had no effect.' As to the propriety of a Vice-President using his office to pressure a Federal agency on behalf of a former crony, the RLA said, 'We treated it like any other communication about a constituent.'

At Agnew's office, Sohmer refused to speak to us, but a spokesman said, 'We regard this very much in the nature of a routine referral. No pressure at all was intended.' In fact, such referrals are 'routine' only from Congressmen. When they come from the White House or Vice-President, they have the earmarks of direct orders.

Footnote: neither the FBI nor the Justice Department has contacted RLA or Maps Inc., in connection with the Federal probe into possible kickbacks given to Agnew and other Maryland political figures.

Jack Anderson

Kerner, Agnew and Justice

You have a judge on the US Circuit Court of Appeals with a lifetime appointment. A gung-ho prosecutor from the opposition party gets a Grand Jury to indict the judge for bribery, fraud, tax evasion and conspiracy.

But hold it, you say! How can the Nixon crowd do that to Judge Otto Kerner? Everybody knows that a prosecutor generally can wheedle an indictment out of a Grand Jury any time he wishes.

Doesn't the Constitution protect Kerner from such 'political' assaults when it requires that a 'civil officer' be impeached before he is indicted and tried in regular courts?

Otto Kerner never used that defense, presumably believing that no jury would convict him. But the jury did find him guilty of crimes dating back to his years as Governor of Illinois, and Kerner was sentenced to three years in prison, a sentence that he has appealed.

Case No. 2. You have a Vice-President of the United States who is accused of taking bribes, kickbacks, extortion money and being involved in related crimes during his tenure as Governor of Maryland.

Except this time the prosecutor is not of the opposing party, but of the Vice-President's own party. There are lots of charges in the press, but an indictment is slow to come from the Grand Jury.

Why? Because in this case the prosecutor isn't sure 'civil officer' Spiro Agnew can be indicted and tried in the courts before he is impeached by Congress.

If we are to believe the leaks coming from sources 'close to the prosecution,' there is ample evidence on which to indict and try Agnew. The only hitch is that Atty. Gen. Elliot Richardson must give the go-ahead. He must decide that either Agnew is indictable and triable for crimes allegedly committed or that the Constitution says Agnew is untouchable unless and until Congress impeaches him.

These two cases ought to make one thing obvious to John Q. Citizen. The Nixon administration cannot read the Constitution one way when it is a Democrat judge it is trying to lock up, yet another way when it is a Republican Vice-President is trying to keep out of the pokey.

The Constitution simply states that 'the President, the Vice-President, and all civil officers of the United States, shall be removed from office on impeachment for, and conviction of, treason, bribery or other high crimes or misdemeanors.'

The Constitution does not give a President or Vice-President any larger sanctuary than any other civil officer. It does not say that a jury can indict and find guilty a judge while a Vice-President remains untouchable.

So if Richardson holds that the Constitution shields Agnew from the Grand Jury he also will have to hold that prosecution of Judge Kerner, which brought such glee to Nixon's aides, was illegal.

It would be a travesty, of course, to hold that the Constitution protects either man from indictment and prosecution for high crimes, especially felonies committed when neither was a 'civil officer' of the Federal government.

And logic rides with those lawyers who argue that the framers of the Constitution never said or meant to imply that the President or any other civil officer must be impeached before he can be tried in the courts for 'treason, bribery or other high crimes or misdemeanors.'

If that were the case, a Franklin D. Roosevelt with a massive Democratic majority could commit the rankest thievery, or even murder, without punishment because 'political loyalty' gave him enough votes to avoid impeachment.

There is no such thing as 'equal justice under the law' when a top civil officer of the Federal government can take bribes, extort money, evade taxes and then hide safely behind the Constitution while a normal bloke gets locked up for half a lifetime for stealing a TV set.

Kerner, Agnew, Bobby Baker, John Ehrlichman and Joe Sikspak all must live or die by the same rules. There is no escape from dictatorship and tyranny when those holding the top reins of power can commit crimes with impunity while the mass of people are constantly under the whip of the law.

Carl T. Rowan

Richardson decides to allow probe

Atty. Gen. Elliot L. Richardson has decided to allow the Federal Grand Jury in Baltimore to begin looking into evidence concerning Vice-President Agnew in its investigation of alleged political kickbacks, according to a highly reliable source.

Richardson has not decided at this time to seek an indictment of the Vice-President, the source emphasized, and the Attorney General still must determine whether there is sufficient evidence to warrant pressing the case and whether any indictment could be issued before the Vice-President was removed from office by impeachment.

The source insisted that 'preliminary steps' can be taken by the Grand Jury in reviewing evidence involving Agnew before Federal prosecutors are allowed to formally present their case to the jury for the purpose of obtaining an indictment.

Justice Department officials last night refused to comment on whether prosecutors may have decided to let persons who have lodged allegations against Agnew in private now appear under oath and be questioned by the Grand Jury.

'In a case of this magnitude, they want to make sure that they are not surprised (by unexpected evidence) and that what a witness says under oath before a Grand Jury is the same as what he says in the prosecutor's office,' the *New York Times* quoted one source as saying.

One figure close to the investigation said it is 'not altogether accurate' to assume that Richardson's assistant in Maryland, US Atty. George Beall, would immediately present evidence that his office is known to have compiled involving the Vice-President.

Although a Grand Jury can review evidence and draw up charges purely on its own authority, any indictment must be signed by a prosecutor – in this case Richardson himself or Beall, acting on behalf of Richardson.

The Attorney General for weeks has considered two questions: Whether there is sufficient evidence to pursue an indictment and whether the Constitution forbids the indictment of an incumbent Vice-President who has not first been removed from office.

Beall last month told Agnew that he was under investigation for possible criminal offenses involving bribery, extortion, conspiracy and violation of Federal tax laws. Agnew has declared his innocence, calling the allegations against him 'damned lies'.

Richardson's permission for the Grand Jury to begin looking into evidence involving the Vice-President was the first formal action involving Agnew since he was informed of the investigation on Aug. 1.

The 22-member Grand Jury has been investigating charges of kickbacks to Maryland politicians from architectural and engineering firms which do business with the state and local governments. Several persons have been furnishing information to Beall in return for limited immunity.

The jury last month returned a 39-count indictment against N. Dale Anderson, who succeeded Agnew as Baltimore County executive in 1967. Anderson yesterday pleaded innocent to the charges, which include bribery, extortion and conspiracy. According to informed sources, the Justice

Department investigation reaches back into Agnew's tenure as Governor of Maryland in 1967 and 1968.

William Taaffe

Agnew departure said discussed

New York (AP) – President Nixon and Vice-President Agnew discussed at their Sept. 1 meeting whether Agnew might resign, according to two sources quoted by *Time Magazine*.

The unnamed sources said Agnew told Nixon he does not want to resign even if indicted by a Baltimore Federal Grand Jury, but the sources, gave conflicting accounts of how Agnew plans to defend himself, *Time* said yesterday.

Spokesmen for Nixon and Agnew previously denied that possible resignation was a topic of the private meeting.

Time quoted one source, a 'friend and adviser' to Agnew, as saying that Agnew has been told by his lawyers that he will be indicated and that Agnew told Nixon he plans to 'fight the indictments head-on in court' without resigning.

Agnew, according to this source, will admit accepting some funds from Maryland contractors and consultants but will argue that the money was used on campaigns and that he promised and gave nothing in return for the donators, *Time* said.

According to the source, Agnew expects to be exonerated by showing that if any favoritism was shown to the contributors while he was Baltimore County Executive or Governor of Maryland it was done by his subordinates, *Time* said.

The other account, provided by 'other sources close to the case,' says Agnew plans to fight the Grand Jury investigation on constitutional grounds, *Time* said.

This posture has upset the tentative timetable of the prosecution since Justice Department officials had expected Agnew to resign, according to the second account.

'The moment he learns that any criminal evidence against him is going to the Grand Jury in Baltimore, his lawyers will lodge formal protests, asking the courts to restrain the Grand Jury,' *Time* reported.

Associated Press

Funneling of cash to Agnew reported

Joel Kline, a multi-millionaire Maryland land investor, has told Federal prosecutors in Baltimore that he acted as a 'conduit' for as much as $100,000 in cash that he allegedly funneled to Agnew and other Maryland officials, according to reliable sources.

Whether Kline gave the money to Agnew and others as political contributions could not be immediately determined.

Kline, considered in 1971 by Gov. Marvin Mandel for the post of Maryland Banking Commissioner, pleaded guilty last month to a charge of conspiring to obstruct a Federal investigation into his business dealings.

Kline, 34, who has offices and residence in Chevy Chase, has also told the prosecutors, according to the sources, that he 'solicited' some of the money personally for the officials as purported campaign contributions.

At the same time, the sources say, Kline has told investigators that he 'laundered some of the money' before it reached the hands of the officials.

By 'laundered,' the sources explained, Kline allegedly manipulated the money in some way to disguise the identity of the original donor.

The sources said that Kline agreed to co-operate with the prosecutors around the time he made his guilty plea and 'he has been talking for weeks.'

Kline was described as one of the latest of the major figures in the investigation of allegations that Agnew and other officials received kickbacks in return for business and personal favors.

The sources said that Kline has named Agnew as one of the recipients of the money he claims to have handled, but it could not be determined how much of the alleged money went to Agnew and whether the alleged funds were given while Agnew was Vice-President or an official in Maryland, where he served as Governor and Baltimore County Executive.

Agnew, under investigation for possible criminal acts of extortion, bribery, tax evasion and conspiracy, has denied all allegations that he received illegal cash payments.

Kline's lawyer, Stephen Sachs, former US Attorney in Baltimore, said yesterday 'I have no comment about a role if any, of Mr Kline in the investigation.'

Jerry Oppenheimer

Bearing down on the high court…

It's beginning to look as if the Supreme Court, whether it wants to or not, is going to be confronted very soon with two of the most momentous decisions it has ever made.

One is whether or not an incumbent Vice-President – and by extension an incumbent President – can be indicted by a Grand Jury, tried and convicted on a criminal offense, without first being impeached by the House of representatives and removed from office by the Senate.

The other is whether or not the courts have the right to compel the release of evidence by the executive branch in a criminal case – in this case, the Watergate tapes – or whether the constitutional separation of powers makes the President immune from any such demand by the judicial branch.

That both of these issues have come to a head at the same time is purely coincidental. The fact that Vice-President Agnew is under investigation for alleged criminal misconduct while he was an official of the State of Maryland is completely unconnected with the Watergate affair. The coincidence is only one more example of the performance of an administration that is calamity prone to a degree that no previous administration has remotely been able to match.

The courts quite certainly and the administration as well would have liked very much to duck these issues. They have, in fact, been ducked successfully for nearly 200 years. Resolving them once and for all is almost certain to cause many problems for future administrations.

Take, for example, the case of the Vice-President.

The White House has been acting recently as if it believed that Spiro Agnew will be indicted on charges that he received kickbacks from people doing business with the government of Maryland. On the basis of what has been said so far, there can be little doubt that the administration would prefer that Agnew resign before his case comes to trial.

If he does, the issue of his invulnerability as a sitting Vice-President to the finding of a Grand Jury will, of course, become moot. Once he has resigned, there is no question that he can be indicted, tried and either convicted or acquitted of any criminal charges exactly as any other American citizen can.

If as seems more likely he does not resign, however, the problem will be inescapable. The Constitution is entirely ambiguous on the question of criminal liability of Presidents or Vice-Presidents – saying only that a Federal official, once he is impeached, convicted and removed from office, can then be tried on criminal charges. The question of whether or not he can be tried before an impeachment proceeding has never been settled by the courts.

At this point, in the light of Agnew's appeal to the House of Representatives to 'investigate' the charges against him, it looks as though the Vice-President is determined to force this issue to a decision. The present indications are that he will challenge the authority of the courts to act against him. In this case, it would be very rash indeed to predict how the Supreme Court might rule. It is equally uncertain how the House will respond to his plea.

The case of the Presidential tapes – though quite separate from the Vice-President's problem – also involves the fundamental issue of executive privilege under the Constitution. The recordings of White House conversations have been demanded by Special Prosecutor Archibald Cox for presentation to the Grand Jury investigating the Watergate affair and by the Senate select committee as well.

So far, the White House has refused to release any of the tapes on the ground that Presidential confidentiality and the principle of the separation of powers would be compromised. Since no agreement has been possible, it appears almost certain that the case also will be carried to the Supreme Court for decision.

The interrelation of the two cases holds fascinating and possibly fearsome implications.

If the court should find that Vice-President Agnew can be tried on criminal charges without first being impeached, the ruling presumably would apply with equal force to the President himself. In this case, with or without the tapes, the Grand Jury could be presented with evidence that Nixon was involved in the Watergate cover-up in the White House – and hence was party to a felony.

On the other hand, if the court rules that Agnew must first be impeached, there is a fairly strong likelihood that impeachment proceedings may be initiated – a process that would take months, if not years. And if the President should defy a court order to release the Watergate tapes, it is at least conceivable that both Nixon and Agnew could find themselves under the threat of impeachment at the same time for quite different reasons.

The fact that this would create an intolerable situation for the country unfortunately is no guarantee that it couldn't happen in the bizarre situation that exists today.

Crosby S. Noyes

Mr Agnew: a stone wall at justice

A miasmic fog of leaks and rumors has obscured the matter of who stands where in the Agnew affair. So it seems useful to set out the basic roles – the more so as an unexpected denouement may emerge.

The White House, as usual, has been trying to shove trouble under the rug. The Vice-President, naturally, has wanted the best break he can get. But the Justice Department – thanks chiefly to a Watergate-burned Assistant Attorney General, Henry Petersen – has been refusing to be party to any fix.

The White House may not have started the rumors of an early resignation by Mr Agnew. But once the word was out, Mr Nixon's men made abundantly clear the President's interest in unloading the Vice-President at the earliest opportunity.

The reason for this unseemly haste is twofold. For one thing, Mr Agnew is a current embarrassment whose troubles underscore and redouble the Watergate difficulties which are already casting such a cloud over the administration.

Moreover with Mr Agnew out, the President would have a chance to designate his successor.

That is important to Mr Nixon not only for the future of the Republican Party. It is important because Mr Nixon would be extremely vulnerable if a Democratic administration took over in 1976. Even a mildly energetic

Democratic Attorney General would probably find, in the dozens of scandals growing out of Watergate, a field day for prosecution.

So, far more than most sitting Presidents, Mr Nixon has a positive interest in having as the next President a Republican deeply in his debt. That is why he is not only pushing the Vice-President to get out, but smoothing the path for John Connally to come in. For Mr Connally would owe almost everything to Mr Nixon, and he could be counted on to turn a blind eye to the wrongs of the present administration.

With no help from the White House, Mr Agnew has had to rely almost entirely on his own resources. His lawyers early blocked out a complicated defense against the charge of accepting bribes and favors. At the heart of the defense was the unresolved constitutional argument that the Vice-President had to be impeached before he could be indicted. The defense posed formidable issues, and it would at least eat up lots of time.

But Mr Agnew was apparently not comfortable with resting his case on such technicalities. Accordingly, his lawyers began talking to the Justice Department about possible arrangements whereby he might give up his legal claims and leave his office in return for concessions by the prosecution.

The Justice Department, however, took a stony attitude. Atty. Gen. Elliot Richardson let the case against various Maryland politicians including Mr Agnew build slowly in Baltimore.

Behind this screen there went forward bargaining between the Agnew lawyers and the Justice Department. The key man was Assistant Atty. Gen. Petersen – a tough prosecutor with a strong sense of right and wrong who worked his way up in the Justice Department from a start as a clerk.

As a strong law-and-order man, Mr Petersen was distinctly unhappy when Ramsey Clark was Attorney General. When John Mitchell came in, Petersen had stars in his eyes. For that reason he was probably more complaisant then he should have been in the early stages of the Watergate investigation.

But when he saw what was going on, Petersen reacted with characteristic energy. He stood up to the President himself, and his threat to resign finally forced Mr Nixon to make one of the big breaks in the Watergate case P the acknowledgment of the burglary on Daniel Ellsberg's psychiatrist.

Petersen has been behaving in the same tough way in the Agnew case. Reliable evidence developed by Fred Graham of CBS shows that Peterson told the Vice-President's lawyers that he had the proof and had it cold. Accordingly, he has been unwilling to go easy on prosecution, even in exchange for a resignation.

At the present writing the upshot is not clear. There could be a quick settlement or a long, complicated litigation. What is clear is that for once, despite the interests of the President and the Vice-President and the administration, the fix was not automatically put in.

Joseph Kraft

The Agnew case: Mr Nixon's options

Unthinking haste characterizes the speculation about what name President Nixon will submit to the Congress as a replacement for Spiro Agnew. Not merely, or even mainly, because the Vice-President has denied reports of imminent resignation.

The true issue is whether Mr Nixon himself is not under a cloud that makes him unfit, at least temporarily, to nominate a new Vice-President. Particularly if it is a matter of in effect, naming now the Presidential nominee who should rightly be selected by the Republican convention in 1976.

The cloud over the President's head is not that vast and tangled mess known as Watergate. It is a very specific issue certain to be resolved one way or another in a month or so. It is the matter of the tapes of his conversations and phone calls.

Archibald Cox, the special Watergate prosecutor, has sought access to these tapes as part of his investigation. The President has refused on the grounds that releasing the tapes to anybody would violate the principle of confidentiality. The issue is now before the courts.

Possibly a new compromise will be struck whereby the White House and the special prosecutor will arrange for some kind of examination as to whether the tapes supply new material relevant in various crimes. If not, the issue will go in the Supreme Court.

The court is due to meet on Oct. 1 and will probably decide the matter by the middle of the month. If it holds against Mr Nixon and the President still refuses to cough up the tapes, the country will be in the presence of serious constitutional crisis. Mr Nixon will have defied the ultimate authority as to the meaning of the Constitution. There will be a prima facie case for impeachment proceedings against him.

In those circumstances, with Mr Nixon himself only a few weeks away from a set of events which could jeopardize his tenure in office, it is against all reason that he designate a successor. It is furthermore against the spirit of the Constitution.

The clear intent of the framers of the Constitution was that in the event of the removal of a President and Vice-President the vacancies be filled by congressional action pending a special election. Article II, section 1, clause 5 provides:

'The Congress may by law provide for the case of removal, death, resignation or inability, both of the President and the Vice-President, declaring what officer shall then act as President, and such officer shall act accordingly, until the disability be removed, or a President shall be elected.'

The various laws of succession, while somewhat ambiguous, also imply that a President under the cloud of impeachment should either clear his name or, in the event no replacement is available, be vindicated or replaced by a special election. It would be inappropriate, accordingly, for the President to rush fences in naming a new Vice-President. The appropriate thing would be for Mr Nixon to wait until the issue of impeachment posed by the tapes is resolved one way or another.

Even then, if Mr Nixon does satisfactorily resolve the issue of tapes, it would be wrong for him to use the appointment of a successor as a means of tilting the Republican nomination of 1976. The country has, in the system of party primaries and party conventions, a well-tested and generally accepted means of making Presidential nominations.

It would be fit, at a time when integrity of government and politics is the central issue of the day, to name someone who is not an aspirant for 1976. The more so as there are large numbers of competent and honorable men in both parties who could clearly fulfill the duties of Vice-President in a credible way that would build the national harmony.

All of this, to be sure, is dry stuff compared to making lists of possible candidates. As a result, political Washington has been almost mute on the subject. But the true need now is for men of solid integrity without any personal ambitions – for example, Majority Leader Mike Mansfield of the Senate – to subordinate the making of lists to an exploration of the ground rules for a fair choice.

Joseph Kraft

Request for probe rejected by Albert
Evidence set for US jury today

Lawyers for Vice-President Spiro T. Agnew are expected to attempt to block a special Federal Grand Jury in Baltimore from beginning to hear evidence against the Vice-President today.

Agnew's lawyers did not file legal papers in Baltimore seeking to block the investigation yesterday, as they had been expected to, but a source close to Agnew said the lawyers' announced intention of raising constitutional objections to the investigation this week 'still stands'.

A knowledgeable legal source said yesterday that if Agnew's lawyers file suit today to halt the investigation, George Beall, the US attorney for Maryland, is expected to withhold evidence against Agnew from the Grand Jury until the constitutional issues of whether a Vice-President can be indicted are resolved.

Barring such a suit, sources said yesterday Federal prosecutors under Beall's direction are prepared to call before the Grand Jury today the first of several witnesses who are expected to detail allegations that Agnew has accepted cash kickbacks from Maryland engineering and architectural firms.

Agnew's precise defense plans and the timing of moves his lawyers are expected to make remained uncertain last night, 24 hours after Attorney General Elliot L. Richardson announced that the Justice Department and Agnew's lawyers had failed to negotiate a settlement of the case that would prevent 'a constitutional dilemma of potentially serious consequence to the nation'.

GRAND JURY SLATED TO TAKE EVIDENCE ON AGNEW TODAY

Richard M. Cohen,
Edward Walsh

Won't act on Agnew note to hill

Speaker Carl Albert rejected yesterday Vice-President Agnew's request for a House investigation of criminal charges swirling around him on grounds that the House should not interfere with matters before the courts.

This setback for Agnew, who had hoped a House inquiry would clear him, came less than 24 hours before the Justice Department is scheduled to begin presenting its evidence of bribery and kickbacks allegedly involving the Vice-President to a Federal Grand Jury in Baltimore today.

Agnew's lawyers did not appear in Federal court there yesterday as expected to try to stop the Grand Jury investigation on grounds that the constitutional separation of powers doctrine bars indictment of a Vice-President while he holds office. They may do so today.

Meanwhile, Agnew denied a White House statement that he and President Nixon had discussed the possibility of Agnew resigning at their meeting Tuesday.

'The President and I have not discussed that possibility,' Agnew told newsmen. 'I want to make it very clear that I am not resigning.'

Albert read the following statement to newsmen and refused to elaborate on it:

'The Vice-President's letter [requesting a House inquiry] relates to matters before the courts. In view of that fact, I, as speaker, will not take any action on the letter at this time.'

Members with whom Albert consulted interpreted this to mean that Albert would oppose the House injecting itself into the case unless the courts should rule they lack the power to try an incumbent Vice-President. And it was generally agreed that as leader of the party that controls the House, Albert has the power to make his decision stick.

Richard L. Lyons

'Toughing it out' for three more years

Remember that slogan of only 10 months ago, 'Four More Years'? Now, in a nightmare reversal of what happened last November, we are to have three more years of dissension and blurred uncertainty over who governs and how.

Those close to the muddled legal process believe Vice-President Spiro Agnew will be in office as his term expires in 1976. If this is proved out, it means that a man subject to indictable offenses of bribery, conspiracy and tax evasion will be one heartbeat away from the Presidency of the United States.

The conjecture on Agnew's staying power, following his refusal to resign his office, is based on the following probabilities. Having wrapped himself in the Constitution by calling on the House of Representatives to investigate the charges against him, he, in effect, is challenging that body to impeach him.

Granting the request, which Speaker Carl Albert summarily rejected, the House would take months to carry out a thorough investigation. It would require a special staff as in the Watergate investigation on the Senate side of the Capital. Merely assembling the relevant material after a committee and a staff have been named would require weeks. Then the fierce glare of the hearings under the television lights could go on for many more weeks.

All this would be preliminary to consideration by the House of a bill of impeachment. Think of the debate with the prospect that each of the 435 members would have something to say. That marathon of labored oratory could be interminable.

In the opinion of this observer the House is unequal to such a challenge. The leadership is fumbling and unsure. While the Democrats have a majority of 150 seats, this includes southerners who have been repeatedly rallied to the Republican side. The emotional response to the plight of a man caught in a web of campaign money and public favors will cut across party lines, since too many of the members themselves know what that kind of tangle means.

So with the avenue of impeachment closed, assuming these probabilities, prosecution in the courts goes forward. Attorney General Elliot L. Richardson has pledged that the allegations against Agnew will be taken before the Grand Jury in Baltimore. But the Vice-President's attorney has raised the shield of the Constitution and that may be protection, if not in the lower court against the threat of a conviction, certainly on the way to the Supreme Court.

This raises the fantastic outlook of the President – on the issue of the tapes – and the Vice-President both refusing the jurisdiction of the courts. Such a defiance of the orderly processes of a government of divided powers can hardly mean less than a breakdown of the system itself.

Sympathy for Agnew has been undoubtedly generated by what has appeared to be a concerted effort through leaks and insinuations of wrongdoing to force him out of office. The widely held belief is that the President wanted to be rid of him so he could name John Connally in his place. Despite repeated denials from the White House and the Justice Department, this belief has persisted.

While sympathy for his plight is understandable, the Vice-President has done little during the first four years to enlist support from other than the stalwarts in his own party. He spent much of the initial two years in a selective attack on the media – an attack believed to have been inspired by the President. In the kind of assignments abroad that have become routine for the No. 2 man he has handled himself capably enough.

After a press conference when the charges against him first surfaced, Agnew went out to stay with his friend Frank Sinatra in Sinatra's luxury empire in Palm Springs, Calif. In light of Sinatra's dubious reputation on several scores this seems a curious retreat. One of his old friends offered this explanation:

'You have to understand that when Nixon tapped him in 1968 in Miami Beach Spiro had never known the big time and the big money. The little money, yes, but not the big. That explains Sinatra and a lot of other things.'

It is the bankruptcy not of an administration or of a man, but of the system itself. The voice of more leadership to point a way out of the morass is still to be heard.

Marquis Childs

Law, order and rights

Beware of poetic justice, which often means one wrong on top of another.

The Nixon administration, for example, has insisted that liberal court decisions and 'soft-headed judges' have elevated the rights of accused persons above the rights of society. No administration has done more to try to make it easier to put people in jail, from its preventive-detention law for the District of Columbia to its widespread use of informers, surveillance, entrapment tactics and grab-bag conspiracy charges.

It may be poetic justice, therefore, but it is still wrong, that the No. 2 man in this grubby 'law and order' administration obviously has been imperiled by the damaging news leaks about his case. It may be tempting to ask where Vice-President Agnew was when J. Edgar Hoover openly accused the Berrigan group of planning to kidnap Henry Kissinger; but that past offense does not justify the present transgressions of those who are making available damaging information on Agnew.

The Agnew charges are one more example of a curious inversion of so-called 'conservative' and 'liberal' attitudes that has been a striking result of Watergate and the Agnew investigation. Few of those who leaped to the defense of Philip Berrigan or the Gainesville Eight have spoken out for the rights of Agnew – any more than he demanded a housecleaning in the Justice Department or the FBI to put an end to such trumped-up cases.

The crux of the Watergate matter, for example, is the misuse of state power to override due process of law and individual rights. The establishment of the 'plumbers' was admittedly an effort to get done by clandestine and unauthorized executive power what could not be done through ordinary and legitimate police operations; since government cannot legally and openly subpoena an accused person's psychiatric records, it set out to steal them.

That is the kind of illicit use of state power to which conservatism, at least in its classic sense, ought to be most strongly opposed. So is the unauthorized tapping of telephones, or the excessive claim to executive secrecy, or the fabrication of documents, whether to distort the historical record of a dead President or to conceal the secret bombing on another country. When such tactics are followed by a 'conservative' administration, true conservatives should be more outraged – because betrayed in principle – than anyone.

Yet, few prominent conservative voices, with honorable exceptions, have been raised against anything but 'excesses' or 'bad judgment' or 'the acts of a few'. The most conservative senators remain silent or find excuses or even defend the White House; and a counterattack has been mounted to show that this strong-arm administration with its contempt for the Bill of Rights is, in fact, the victim of liberals and the press.

On the other hand, liberals seem all too complaisant, even happy, about the difficulties in which Nixon and Agnew find themselves. Few liberals, in the case of Nixon, have come forward to sat that, however his administration may have abused its powers, it was 'strong' Democratic Presidents who did the most to expand the Presidency to its present imperial status. Nor have liberal Democrats – again with honorable exceptions – been willing to conclude that, although Nixon in his security mania may have carried the doctrine of implied powers out the window, that doctrine is primarily the product of liberal Democratic thought and policy and ultimately was bound to lead to abuse.

This is not a justification for Watergate or any other excessive uses of state power; it ought to be a warning, however, that liberal Democrats will not automatically end the threat to liberty inherent in the imperial Presidency merely by coming back to power in 1976. Their own doctrines need as much re-examination as the perversions of them sponsored by the Nixon administration.

Sadly enough, the truth may be that 'conservatives' have become too willing to skimp their traditional insistence on individual rights in their overriding concern for law and order at home and anti-communism abroad; while 'liberals' have been too willing to sacrifice individual rights to their desire for the kind of social reform that could only be achieved at least in the short run – by state power centered in the Presidency.

But at least Watergate and the Agnew case have exposed ideology in America, on both ends of the political spectrum, as being mostly a matter of whose ox is gored; and they have suggested that, when it comes to individual rights against the power of the state, neither right nor left has much reason to set itself up above the other. These are small, but not unimportant, victories in the war against hypocrisy.

Tom Wicker

Agnew declares he won't resign even if indicted

Los Angeles, Sept. 29 – Vice-President Agnew vowed today that he would remain in office even if he is indicted, and he accused top Justice Department officials of attempting to destroy him politically with 'malicious and outrageous' news leaks.

A wildly cheering audience of 2,000 Republican women interrupted Agnew with applause 32 times as the Vice-President proclaimed his innocence of accusations that he got kickbacks from Maryland contractors.

He singled out Assistant Attorney General Henry E. Petersen, accusing him of attempting to rescue through an Agnew prosecution a reputation lost through 'ineptness and blunder' in the Watergate and other cases.

'Because of the tactics that have been employed against me, because small and fearful men have been frightened into giving evidence against me... I will not resign if indicted,' Agnew said.

[In Washington, Attorney General Elliot L. Richardson praised Petersen and said Agnew had 'singled out for criticism a career public servant constrained from defending himself by the ethical standards governing a criminal investigation.']

The delegates to the National Federation of Republican Women's convention yelled their approval of Agnew's statement and stood on tables to cheer. The waved programs, scarves and signs that said, 'Spiro My Hero' and

'Agnew for President'. Above the cheering Agnew said once more: 'I will not resign if indicted.'

Agnew's emotional defense of his innocence came as an addition to a far blander prepared text in which he philosophically discussed the necessity of Grand Jury secrecy and referred only once to his own case, calling it a 'cruel form of kangaroo trial in the media'.

When he finished his prepared text, the Vice-President looked directly at the television cameras and said he had decided to add some remarks because of the opportunity offered by national television.

'In the past several months I have been living in purgatory,' Agnew began, 'I have found myself the recipient of undefined, unclear and unattributed accusations that have surfaced in the largest and most widely circulated organs of our communications media. I want to say at this point – clearly and unequivocally – I am innocent of the charges against me.'

Agnew was drowned out by applause and cries of 'Right on.' He continued above the din, proclaiming that he had not 'used my office nor abused my public trust, as County Executive, as Governor or as Vice-President.'

Lou Cannon

Agnew's assault

We are witness to strange new twists of law and politics, as this country begins to explore uncharted constitutional questions that will affect, most vitally, the two highest officials of the land. Vice-President Agnew's assault on the Justice Department of the administration in which he is the second highest member was something without parallel in living memory. Quite obviously, the internal collision with the Nixon administration is as jolting and debilitating as any experienced with outside forces. Agnew is hitting hard and he isn't slugging at Democratic senators, but instead is seeking whatever relief he can find in the Democratic controlled House of Representatives.

Most Americans, we expect, were left more bewildered than ever by his scathing speech last Saturday, in which he charged that high officials of Justice had set out to ruin him politically with 'malicious and outrageous' news leaks. And why would they want to do anything so seemingly irrational? The Vice-President indicated it was because Assistant Attorney General Henry E. Petersen, having muffed the Watergate investigation through 'ineptness and blunder' wants to recoup a prosecutorial reputation. Agnew sees himself as the 'big trophy' in this alleged plot of Petersen and others. But the final decision to proceed with a Federal investigation of Agnew, related to allegations of criminal misconduct when he was Governor of Maryland – and in one instance since then – surely was made above Petersen's level. This went to the top, undoubtedly, and both Attorney

General Richardson and the White House have come to Petersen's defense. He did not, they think, put out a leak last month that Justice has the 'cold' goods on the Vice-President.

The harsh fact remains, though, that leaks about the investigation and Grand Jury activities in Baltimore have been numerous and to Agnew's great detriment. In all likelihood, his political career has been destroyed. He deserves much sympathy for being the victim of a vast seepage of disclosure and speculation about his predicament from unidentified sources. His anger at this is fully understandable, and shared by many citizens who want to see justice done. But perhaps he is giving the Justice Department altogether too much blame for the leakage, which has come from diverse places.

In any case, the national interest demands that a way be found to cut through all the rhetoric and rumor as quickly as possible. Questions that involve integrity at the summits of our public life cannot be left in lengthy suspense, without a great deal more loss of public faith in government. In Agnew's case, it is the evidence that counts, and this must be unfolded publicly in its entirety. His legal effort to prevent criminal proceedings against him in court, on the grounds of constitutional immunity, offers a dismal prospect. It could delay intolerably the final accounting which the country desperately needs. By far the best alternative is the one Agnew himself offered last week – a full and speedy investigation by the House of Representatives, to give the public and the Congress every fact needed to decide on his guilt or innocence and consequently, whether he Vice-President Agnew remains in office. We hope the House leadership will reconsider its hasty rejection of this proposal.

Editorial Comment
The *Star News*

Mr Agnew's California speech

There are no atheists in foxholes and, as it seems, there are no anti-civil libertarians under criminal investigation. We listened to the Vice-President's eloquent assertion of the rights of the accused the other day, just as we have listened to various administration Watergate defendants' assertions of the importance of their constitutional rights, and only wished that these men had been as eloquent on the subject when the rights of others were at stake. How good – and how important – it would have been to hear Mr Agnew's disquisition, say, in the wake of the Mayday troubles or on the eve of the Panther trial in New Haven. Saturday, the Vice-President told a nationwide TV audience that he did not believe he could get a 'fair hearing' before a Grand Jury or a petite jury in Baltimore because the 'well has been most successfully poisoned'. Three years ago when President Kingman Brewster of Yale suggested that black revolutionaries could not get a fair hearing under our judicial system, Vice-President Agnew recommended that he be fired.

Let us be clear about this: so far as his new found commitment to certain constitutional protections of the individual is concerned, Vice-President Agnew is on sound ground. What makes his California speech so troubling is the fact that he now seems determined to exploit and cheapen these very serious concerns with the same kind of reckless, self-serving political rhetoric that marked his earlier forays into national political life – a technique, incidentally, which he disavowed in the 1972 campaign as having been foisted upon him. It was one thing for Mr Agnew a short while back to complain about those leaks and indiscretions which were bringing supposedly secret investigatory material to public attention. It is quite another for him to mount a personal attack on the head of the Justice Department's Criminal Division, Mr Henry Petersen, suggesting that Mr. Petersen is pursuing this investigation only for base reasons of self-interest. When the Vice-President contends that the prosecutors in his case are corrupt and that the witnesses against him are self-serving perjurers – adding, in passing, that Mr Petersen is an incompetent loser of cases – he can hardly be said to be striking a blow for orderly process or the dignity of the system of justice or the rights of the accused. He can only be said to be trying to manipulate public opinion in his favor at the expense of anything in his way.

Surely Mr Agnew must realize that opinion in this country is very mixed and uncertain on the subject of his present dilemma. People who do not count themselves among his natural constituency or his usual admirers, are troubled by the manner in which the case against him seemed so suddenly to materialize and by its relationship to the President's own troubles and by the clearly Byzantine atmosphere within the administration surrounding Mr Agnew's plight. And they are troubled by those erosions of his rights as the object of a criminal inquiry.

On this score, the Vice-President has every right to be 'powerfully annoyed,' as we put it some weeks ago at the start of this affair, if those in charge of the investigation have acted carelessly or unprofessionally. But two wrongs will not set this matter right. If Mr Agnew wishes to demonstrate his own seriousness, responsibility and good faith, and to the advantage of the reservoir of genuine concern that exists, he will not do so by indulging the kind of cynical, contemptuous and defiant nonsense that he made use of in his Saturday speech. If he is genuinely concerned about undocumented allegations made against him by nameless accusers or by anonymous second-hand sources, he does little credit to his argument by replying in kind. It is one thing for him to claim – and rightly so – the rights and presumptions accorded the ordinary citizen. It is quite another for him to exploit his high office by means not available to ordinary citizens in an effort to fire up a partisan constituency in his behalf. There is more than one way, in short, to generate prejudicial pre-trial publicity.

What is urgently needed now, in our view, is less talk about unfairness – for there has been unfairness on both sides of this case – and the speediest possible resolution of the matter in the courts of law. It is only by way of orderly safeguarded processes of justice that Mr Agnew can get his due: a fair and conclusive determination of the merit of any charges made against him. The Vice-President has complained that those processes are being undermined by the behavior of the prosecution. Precisely the same can be said of his own attempt to avoid the jurisdiction of the courts to take refuge behind the claims of constitutional immunities allegedly inherent in his office, and to cast doubt on the integrity and the motives of attorneys and prospective witnesses.

Editorial Comment
The Star News

Agnew's plight

There is reason to feel sorry for Spiro Agnew in his present plight. Not that the Vice-President has been unfairly done in by the Justice Department, as he and his supporters seem pleased to believe. The true sadness lies in the circumstances which finds the Vice-President of the United States totally unfitted by experience to meet the troubles which beset him.

Two incidents demonstrate the Vice-President's incapacity for dealing effectively with is present affairs. One is the bold claim that he will not resign even if indicted by the Grand Jury in Baltimore. Nobody aware of the realities of life in Washington could advance that claim.

If Mr Agnew is indicted, the President could be obliged by solemn public commitments to force him out. At a minimum, Mr Nixon would cut off all the Vice-President's delegated functions. There would be no missions abroad, no service on various boards and commissions, no office in the White House complex – not even a telephone in the executive branch.

The Vice-President could, of course, go up to Capital Hill to fulfill his constitutional duty of presiding over the Senate. But Mr Agnew has few friends in the Senate. He gave up presiding regularly over that body years ago when he was stung by a harsh comment made during the debate over the Anti-Ballistics Missile, or ABM.

The hard ball players in the Senate are already rubbing their hands over the fun they would have at Mr Agnew's expense if he came back. Day after day they would be sarcastically congratulating Mr Agnew on the floor for having learned his constitutional duties from a Grand Jury.

It would be the kind of punishment nobody could withstand – least of all a man as personally sensitive as the Vice-President. Once that is taken into account, Mr Agnew's claim that he would stay in office even if indicted is shown up as the merest bravado.

A second revealing incident was the Vice-President's request last week that the House of Representatives move in to consider his case before it went to the Grand Jury. The request was made in extreme haste, without any preparation of Speaker Carl Albert or other Democratic leaders.

But anybody who knows anything about Washington knows one thing. It is that getting congressional approval for a controversial matter requires the most laborious preparation of key figures behind the scenes.

Without such careful laying of the ground, the Congress merely follows its natural instinct. The natural instinct is to duck hard cases. If nothing else, Speaker Albert and his men are world champions in rolling down the hill whatever is rolled up to them. Which is precisely what they did, and in a matter of hours, with the Vice-President's request.

The reason why the Vice-President is so ill-equipped for his present difficulties is clear. Most men in American politics move up gradually from office to office. They acquire knowledge and experience. They come to know instinctively what is possible and not possible in a given circumstance.

But the rise of the Vice-President has been by mere fluke. He was hand-picked by Mr Nixon to be Vice-President. Before that he had served only two years as Governor of the small state of Maryland. He was elected largely thanks to a crazy Democratic primary.

Before becoming Governor, Mr Agnew was for four years Chief Executive of Baltimore County. But he owed that post also to a freak division in the democratic Party. Thus the Vice-President did not face the crises and problems usual to American politicians. He did not come to political responsibility with even the nominal equipment of the self-made man.

President Nixon could have changed that. He could have trained the Vice-President up. He could have given him important diplomatic assignments. He could have given him true domestic responsibilities.

But the President chose to use his Vice-President purely as a stump speaker and fund raiser. Mr Agnew has transacted no piece of serious foreign business. He knew and knows nothing of the negotiations with Russia or China.

Nor did he have any serious part in domestic affairs. The making of the budget is a mystery to him. He is blind to the intricacies of legislation, and deaf to the moods of the Congress.

He now finds himself totally unprepared to meet the crisis of his life. He is making wild, demonstrably inaccurate charges about the Department of Justice. He is appealing to a Congress that has almost no sympathy for his case. He is posturing before the press and the public in a way that is going to make him look ridiculous.

It is a sad spectacle. Perhaps the saddest aspect of it is that Mr Agnew is not alone. Like John Mitchell and John Ehrlichman and Bob Haldeman he is a man not much better or worse than most. Like them, he is in way over his head, thanks chiefly to Richard Nixon.

Joseph Kraft

Agnew: 'hanged without a trial'

Unless you are either totally devoid of feeling or totally convinced of his guilt, you have to have at least a little sympathy for Vice-President Agnew.

The odds are against his having anything like a fair trial on the charges now, apparently, about to be made against him. And there is no chance whatever that he will survive the ordeal with his reputation and his honor intact – no matter if he never accepted a single bribe, did a dishonest favor or took an unwarranted dollar.

Agnew the politician is dead already, and Agnew the human being is close to it. In both cases, the fate may be deserved. The point is, he's been hanged without a trial.

No, that's a wrong figure; he's been drowned in a dambreak of leaks.

It is difficult for a politician to survive even the accusation of graft – especially a politician so high in the Government. The natural assumption was that even the letter informing Agnew that he was under investigation would not have been written unless there was fairly solid evidence against him. Maybe that's not fair, either, but it's forgivable.

What isn't forgivable, in the name of justice, is that so many unchecked and uncheckable particulars of the allegations against him were made public, primarily through leaks to newsmen. For as a result, there is no longer simply a suspicion of wrongdoing hanging over his head; it has come to the point where many people only wonder how much graft he took, not whether he took it.

And because he already stands condemned without a trial, it strikes me as particularly harsh to chide him, as some have, for backing away from his earlier statement of 'confidence in the criminal justice system of the United States'.

He asserted that confidence last month when he made his decision to meet head-on charges against him. He said then that he expected to be vindicated in the courts. But that was before he was convicted in the streets. When that situation changed, so did Agnew's chances of any meaningful vindication, except, perhaps, for staying out of jail.

Thus it does not seem unreasonable for him to be asking now that the House of Representatives air the charges against him – even publicly, on television, if it wants to. It is inconsistent, to be sure, particularly in light of his earlier condemnation of the Watergate hearings as complicating, not facilitating, the search for truth.

Because of the charges already floating around, many of which have been accepted as fact by too many of us, acquittal in court will have very little meaning so far as Agnew's reputation is concerned, unless he is able to prove beyond any doubt that all the charges are false. That seldom happens in any trial. What is more likely is that acquittal would come on a finding of insufficient evidence, reasonable doubt, inadmissibility of evidence or some such.

Any such outcome would keep him out of jail, but not much more. And the failure of the Grand Jury to indict him, for any reason at all, would fix his wagon good. For in that case, we'd all 'know' he was guilty.

The congressional investigation Agnew has begged for wouldn't guarantee fairness, but it may offer the best possibility of it. The nature of the hearings is such that the public can get a clearer idea of what is going on than in a courtroom, with all the talk of objections and citations and precedents.

On TV you get a better look at the accused and the accusers, and you're able to form more satisfactorily opinions as to who is to be believed. Agnew seems to think he could be convincing in such a forum – not that it would revive Agnew the politician; he's given up on that. But it might help rescue Agnew the man.

It shouldn't be necessary to say that this is neither an attack on the courts nor a brief for Spiro Agnew. An important aspect of the judicial system that Agnew once declared so much faith in is its provisions for an orderly disclosure of evidence, with opportunity for examination and cross-examination of witnesses, and challenges of their credibility. The courts, that is to say, are supposed to offer protection against what already has happened to Agnew.

As to the man itself, I personally don't care for him. And to be perfectly honest about it, I am not at all convinced that he is innocent of graft.

By the same token, some of the black victims of Old South lynch mobs may actually have forcibly raped white women. But guilt is no justification for lynching.

If Agnew, is as guilty as many of us believe he is, we shouldn't be afraid to have it come out – the right way.

William Raspberry

Nixon calls Agnew move 'proper' one

President Nixon said yesterday that he regarded Vice-President Spiro T. Agnew's decision not to resign if indicted as 'an altogether proper one,' but added that the allegations concerning Agnew are 'serious and not frivolous'.

While insisting that he 'respected' Agnew's intention not to quit, Mr Nixon declined to endorse the Vice-President's criticism of Assistant Attorney General Henry E. Petersen.

Agnew charged in Los Angeles last Saturday that Petersen was a source of 'malicious and outrageous' news leaks that had prejudiced Agnew's chances of receiving a fair trial on allegations that he violated felony, bribery, conspiracy and extortion statutes when he was Governor of Maryland or Baltimore County Executive.

The Vice-President said that the Justice Department was trying to get him as 'a trophy' so that Petersen could recover a reputation damaged in the Government investigation of the Watergate case.

Mr Nixon said yesterday that he would have removed Petersen if there was 'clear evidence that he had been guilty of an indiscretion'. The President went on to say that Attorney General Elliot L. Richardson had assured him that an investigation within the Justice Department had determined that Petersen had not been responsible for the news leaks.

The President, at a relaxed and informal new conference praised Agnew for 'distinguished service as Vice-President,' and urged that he not be 'tried and convicted by the press and on television by leaks and innuendoes' in the present 'white-hot atmosphere'. But as he has on other occasions, Mr Nixon drew a distinction between Agnew's service as Vice-President and as Maryland Governor.

'...The charges that have been made against him do not relate in any way to his activities as Vice-President of the United States,' Mr Nixon said.

Lou Cannon

The impeachment – first approach

A considerable injustice, it seems to me, is being done to Vice-President Agnew in accusing him of tricky legalistic maneuvers in order to frustrate the course of justice in the case of criminal charges made against him.

One way or another, Agnew is going to get exactly what is coming to him – either conviction or vindication. And no amount of legal maneuvering is likely to change the outcome one way or the other.

Agnew is reproached particularly for taking the stand that, under the Constitution, he cannot be tried for a criminal offense unless he is first impeached by the House, tried by the Senate and dismissed from office. The assumption is made that this would be a hard and time-consuming process and that his chances of acquittal would be better than before an ordinary jury.

In fact, it would have been most remarkable if the Vice-President had not insisted on the impeachment-first approach. Indeed, it may not have been entirely his own idea. The line is wholly consistent with President Nixon's concept of the separation of powers and his own refusal to accept the jurisdiction of the courts in the matter of the Watergate tapes. A failure by Agnew to challenge the jurisdiction of the courts would have amounted to a serious defection from firm administration doctrine.

In any event, the constitutional challenge has been made and it will have to be settled one way or another by the

Supreme Court. Essentially, it is a question of interpreting ambiguous language in the Constitution. There is no particular reason to suppose that a decision will take an inordinate amount of time, and it is extremely difficult to see how it could be indecisive. Either a sitting Vice-President can be indicted, tried and convicted or acquitted in court, or he cannot. There is no possible compromise on the issue that a layman can discern.

Nor is there any presumption that the Court will decide in Agnew's favor. A ruling that the Vice-President is answerable to the courts no doubt would have far-reaching consequences for this and future administrations. But so would one that established once and for all a doctrine of complete executive invulnerability.

A ruling against Agnew on the constitutional issue would mean that he could be tried like any other citizen. If he should be convicted, there almost certainly would be no need for any impeachment proceedings. It is inconceivable that in those circumstances the Vice-President would not resign forthwith.

If, on the other hand, the Court should uphold Agnew's position and rule that he must be dismissed by impeachment before he can be tried, it is equally inconceivable to me that impeachment proceedings would not immediately be instituted. The refusal of the House last week to launch its own investigation of the charges against the Vice-President quite clearly did not reflect any reluctance to deal with the matter, but simply a feeling that the legal problem should be disposed of first.

It is highly premature to speculate on how the Vice-President would fare in a congressional proceeding. The presumption that politicians would be inclined to take it easy on one of their own kind is at least open to considerable doubt. It may be, as Agnew has suggested, that members of Congress would be more 'sophisticated' than an ordinary jury when it comes to the question of kickbacks and campaign money. But if the charges are anything like as solid as the Justice Department says they are, I would suspect that Agnew is in for a rough time, whatever forum may consider his case.

The Vice-President certainly is right in believing that he is a dead duck so far as his political future is concerned and well justified in his resentment at how his demise has been brought about. He is wrong, however, at least in part, in laying the blame on top Justice Department officials. At least some of the 'leaks' that he complains of having come from people with no connection whatever with the Government.

If his case should be dumped back into the lap of the Congress, it is important to remember what will be at stake. The House – and perhaps subsequently the Senate – will be hearing evidence on criminal charges against the Vice-President. But essentially they will be passing judgment on his fitness to remain in office for the next three years. And that is the essential issue that confronts the country at this point.

Crosby S. Noyes

Agnew to keep speaking out
Taking 'Case to the Country'

Vice-President Spiro T. Agnew was described yesterday as convinced that he must 'take his case to the country' in the hope of winning it eventually in Congress.

Two supporters of the Vice-President, one an Agnew aide and the other a Republican Party official, said that Agnew has come to the conclusion that he ultimately will face some sort of congressional proceeding arising from the accusation compiled by government prosecutors. These supporters said that Agnew believes he can convince a majority of the American people that he is innocent and, further, that Congress will be receptive to public opinion.

Another person in the Agnew camp said the Vice-President is so convinced that he will be exonerated that he is already looking ahead to the 1974 Congressional campaign. In his meeting with California Republican officials in Los Angeles last Saturday – where Agnew said it would 'not be realistic' for him to consider himself a Presidential possibility in 1976 the Vice-President also discussed party prospects in next year's elections.

That closed door meeting came immediately after Agnew's emotional speech to the convention of the National Federation of Women. The Vice-President was drowned out by applause when he declared that he had been accused on perjured testimony and would not resign if indicted.

Lou Cannon

Agnew to fight validity of probe

Vice-President Agnew's lawyers plan to file legal papers in Federal court this week seeking to block investigation of him by a Federal Grand Jury in the Maryland political corruption inquiry, close associates of Agnew say.

Agnew's lawyers expect to file the papers in US District Court in either Washington or Baltimore challenging the constitutionality of a Grand Jury's investigation or indicting a sitting Vice-President, the associates say.

Agnew also has started forming his own 'legal defense fund,' and these associates say that and the upcoming court action are proof he plans to 'fight out' charges against him and is making no deals with Federal prosecutors.

At the same time, Agnew lawyers and associates emphatically denied published reports yesterday quoting Capitol Hill sources as saying Agnew's lawyers are conducting 'plea bargaining' sessions with top Justice Department officials.

According to reports circulating in the Capital Friday, the lawyers and officials allegedly discussed a possible resignation by Agnew in return for his being allowed to plead guilty to a minor offense.

'There is no foundation to these stories,' said a legal spokesman for Agnew who is familiar with his strategy. 'There has been no plea bargaining.' He said the reports 'are just part of this superheated atmosphere' surrounding Agnew's case.

Associates said the precise direction of the legal papers to be filed this week 'has not been completely set'. But one emphasized that 'the papers are consistent with the contention that a Grand Jury cannot investigate a sitting Vice-President or hand up an indictment against him'.

While there were strong indications that there were discussions between Agnew lawyers and Justice department officials last week, associates of Agnew indicated it was the constitutional issue and not plea bargaining that was the topic.

Jerry Oppenheimer,
Ronald Sarro

Agnew's letter

Following is the text of Vice-President Agnew's letter yesterday to Atty. Gen. Elliot L. Richardson:

Dear Mr. Attorney General:

On August 6, 1973, you met with me in my office and sketchily informed me of the general nature of certain allegations being investigated by the United States Attorney's Office in Baltimore.

I appreciated your affording me this courtesy. I understand this is the practice of the Department with respect to the investigation of any subject whose co-operation is requested.

As you know, since April I have consistently offered United States Attorney George Beall my complete co-operation.

I expected after our meeting that personnel of the Department of Justice would assiduously fulfill their obligation to pursue the inquiry. Indeed, I welcomed and have sought the fullest investigation. Making good on my offer of co-operation, I have made my records available to Mr Beall and have volunteered for personal interview.

I expected that the investigation would be conducted not only thoroughly, but secretly, with the usual safeguards of possible Grand Jury proceedings. Tragically, the safeguards have been virtually non-existent.

I am sure I need not recount for you the constant blow of published stories attributed to 'sources close to the investigation' and 'Justice Department sources'. Time Magazine yesterday, in fact, liberally quoted unnamed Justice Department officials.

In view of this history, there can be no question that some personnel of your Department have regularly released information to the press – when their duty was to maintain silence.

There can be no doubt that you now have the obligation to investigate these leaks and to use all the tools at your disposal to expose and discipline those responsible. Only drastic and immediate action will curb this vicious and illegal practice.

Of course, I am concerned about the impact of these leaks upon me and upon the office I hold. I am equally concerned, however, with the impact which the extensive publicity may have on others – especially private citizens – who may also be subjects of the investigation. It would be a dreadful injustice if their rights were to be prejudiced simply because they are caught in the swirl of publicity created by the charges, rumors, speculations and leaks involving me.

Let me dispose of one rumor – that I have encouraged this stream of leaks as part of my defense strategy. This is malicious nonsense. Indeed, in view of the prejudicial character of the leaks and their regular attribution to Justice Department sources, the rumor is inherently absurd.

I sincerely hope that you will take immediate steps to stop this gross perversion of justice. The American people have a right to insist not only upon determined investigation of criminal charges, but also upon investigatory processes which safeguard the rights of those involved. I, as Vice-President, and you, as Attorney General, share a common responsibility in this regard, a responsibility which I have endeavored to discharge since I first became aware of the investigation.

Sincerely,
Spiro T. Agnew

Editorial Comment
The *Star News*

The amazing, gutsy Richardson

Vice-President Spiro Agnew's troubles with the law have dramatized anew the truism that 'justice' is too important to entrust to crass politicians.

We Americans have known that for years, yet we have watched meekly as Presidents of both parties have put campaign managers and chief political advisers in the job of Attorney General of the Untied States.

A lot of Americans (including democrats, not the least being Lyndon B. Johnson) were deeply distrustful of the fair and impartial workings of justice with Robert F. Kennedy running the Justice Department.

Even more people regarded it as an outrage that John N. Mitchell should be in a position to decide who got bugged or wiretapped, who got indicted and who got prosecuted with how much fervor – because his chief claim to the Attorney Generalship was his service as Richard Nixon's campaign manager.

But now we see Elliot L. Richardson putting on an amazing exhibition of the kind of independent, gutsy regard for the law that Americans ought always demand from an Attorney General.

It is almost incredible that a Republican Attorney General should move so doggedly toward the possible indictment and even imprisonment of a Republican Vice-President.

Richardson apparently is moving relentlessly against Agnew out of a conviction that the institutions of justice in

American cannot withstand what the public would regard as another bald attempt to cover up high-level crime.

Agnew suggests that what the Justice Department is trying to do to him is the rankest sort of politics – that Henry Petersen and others in Justice are trying to kill him off as the 'big trophy' which will make the American people forget how they bungled the Watergate investigation.

Some of Agnew's friends go further and suggest that Richardson may be the most venally political of all Attorneys General because he is leading a 'plot' to focus national attention on Agnew and make the public forget Watergate.

This argument loses plausibility for one over powering reason: The same Justice Department that plunged the President into a grave crisis over the Watergate tapes.

Richardson is to be commended for knowing that he could stand so firmly without being driven out of office.

The President had called on him when the administration of the State Department was in a mess; when the huge, chronically mismanaged Department of Health, Education and Welfare was leaderless; when the hopelessly wasteful and ungovernable Department of Defense needed a new boss, and, finally, when the Justice Department became critical to the maintenance of even a shred of public faith in the workings of this administration.

Richardson leaped out with courage when Agnew assailed his deputies, including Petersen. Richardson stated emphatically that he is making the decisions as to the Agnew prosecution, and that if Agnew's followers want to 'get' anyone he is the man they must go after.

This Boston Brahmin Richardson, who can seem cold and colorless, with nothing of the bombastic rhetoric so typical of Agnew, or the egotistical flair so common to John Connally, may turn out to be a hard man to 'get.'

Carl T. Rowan

Mr Agnew and the Vice-Presidency

The one meaningful duty of the Vice-Presidency is a contingent one which may not occur during the tenure of any one incumbent. But it is no less vital to the country on that account, because that one duty simply stated is to pick up the burdens of the Presidency at a time of extraordinary national stress. This imposes upon a Vice-President a continuing obligation that is quiet different from the requirement upon every citizen – including the Vice-President – to obey the law. It is the Vice-President's sworn duty to uphold the law.

Similarly, the obligations imposed upon a Vice-President demand more of him than simply that he be innocent of a crime. For the effective discharge of his responsibility as a stand-in to the Presidency, he must not even appear to be guilty of wrongdoing – to hold himself free, in other words, of any taint which would rob his office and himself of public confidence. It is in this light that one must examine not the allegations which have been raised against Mr Agnew in recent months – for no formal charges have been placed against him – but his response to original official notification that he was the target of an investigation and his subsequent twists and turns in his defense as it developed once it began to appear that this investigation might lead to his indictment on criminal charges.

From the beginning, Mr Agnew embarked on a vigorous and skillful defense. As soon as it became known that he was formally the subject of a Federal criminal investigation, he issued a statement in which he declared, 'I am innocent of any wrongdoing... I have confidence in the criminal justice system of the United States and... I am equally confident my innocence will be affirmed'.

Shortly thereafter, he summoned the press to a conference which was televised nationally. He told the nation, 'I have nothing to hide'. He also disclosed that as soon as he had heard rumors of the investigation and stories that he was trying to impede it, he sent his lawyer to George Beall, the United States Attorney in Baltimore, to make assurances that he, Mr Agnew, had no intention of blocking the investigation. Although he did not rule out a resort to constitutional arguments, Mr Agnew in early August gave every appearance that he was prepared to deal with his problems in the only acceptable way for a man in his office – that is to say, quickly, cleanly and openly.

Then, after several quiet weeks, came reports of private conversations between Mr Agnew's lawyers and the Department of Justice. Attorney General Richardson has now confirmed that such conversations did take place. Though both parties attempted to keep the substance of the talks private, the essence of those discussions became public and it disclosed that the Vice-President's 'confidence in the criminal justice system' had apparently collapsed. All the evidence suggests, in fact, that he was prepared to bargain away his high office in exchange for the dropping of all or most of the charges against him. When negotiations broke down, and the Department of Justice decided to present its evidence about Mr Agnew to the Baltimore Grand Jury, the Vice-President then appealed to the House of Representatives. That body, he claimed, was the only one which could carry out the kind of investigation contemplated by the Constitution for civil officers of the Government. The measure of his retreat from his professed faith in the criminal justice system – and from his earlier publicly-stated distrust of congressional investigations – can best be seen in what he had to say about the Senate Watergate Committee only a few weeks ago. The Congressional investigation, the Vice-President said 'tends to complicate the search for truth by making both witnesses and (the) committee players on a spotlighted national stage'. He also said such investigations had 'Perry Masonish impact' which made the public the ultimate judges of facts which should be heard before the court.

The move to the House gives us a good notion of the desperate position at which Mr Agnew has lately arrived. It is consistent with his lawyers' view that he has to be impeached by the House and removed by the Senate before he can be indicted for criminal conduct. It is, in short, a clever maneuver, because if the Vice-President's legal argument prevails and if, for whatever reason the Congress thereupon fails to remove him by impeachment, Mr Agnew could not be convicted of a crime until his term of office expires and the statute of limitations has run out on many if not all of the charges that might be placed against him.

Now this, we would acknowledge, is an entirely proper legal strategy for any private citizen engaged in a fight to avoid indictment or conviction for criminal activity. It may well be precisely the right sort of maneuvering and the best possible course of action if the objective is nothing more than to spare the Vice-President from going to jail. But precisely what would be right and reasonable about this strategy for a private citizen is what is wrong about it for the Vice-President of the United States. For what the Vice-President has clearly conveyed in the course of his various shifts of position is that he is not, in the last analysis, prepared to place his confidence in the judicial process, that he does not want to allow his case to move through the Grand Jury proceedings toward a possible indictment or conviction, that he is in fact prepared to seize upon whatever legal device may come to hand in order to prevent any of these things from happening. On the contrary, it appears that his lawyers are poised to put their case for impeachment as a precondition to indictment to the test of the Federal judiciary, now that the Speaker of the House has wisely and correctly refused to grant him the special inquiry he requested Tuesday afternoon.

And so, presumably, we are confronted with a protracted and quite possibly inconclusive battle in the courts – not over the Vice-President's innocence or guilt, not over anything, in fact, that would serve to clear his name or to satisfy public doubts, but over a procedural, constitutional issue which can only delay that quick, clear answer which a man in his high official position ought to wish to provide as a matter of course. For Spiro T. Agnew, as citizen of the United States and entitled to all its protections under law, it is a sensible and perhaps even a sound strategy. For Spiro T. Agnew, Vice-President of the United States, it is a strategy so contrived, evasive and insensitive to the real issues at stake as to raise serious questions, of and by itself, about his continuing fitness for the high office he holds.

Editorial Comment
The *Washington Post*

Goldwater's warning

Sen. Barry Goldwater, the conservative Republican elder whose advice on the Agnew affair is widely respected, has privately warned President Nixon through intermediaries that a Vice-Presidential vacancy would be no blessing either for the President or his party.

Goldwater declines to confirm or deny that he has discussed the Agnew affair with the White House. In truth, however, the senator specifically told Mr Nixon that either Gov. Nelson Rockefeller or John B. Connally would 'split the GOP' if named to succeed Agnew.

He was reacting to widespread reports of the White House plotting Agnew's early exit, thus giving Mr Nixon the opportunity not only to anoint his successor but also to pull public attention off Watergate by naming a new Vice-President. Not so. Goldwater is said by high party officials to have warned the White House, if Agnew resigned, Mr Nixon could not name a prospective 1976 Republican Presidential candidate without doing serious damage to the Republican Party. The reason: party factions controlled by a leader not named to the vacancy would resent the new Vice-President having a long leg up on the 1976 nomination. Consequently, creation of a vacancy in the Vice-Presidency during a time that the President himself is at so low an ebb of popularity could splinter the party.

Rowland Evans,
Robert Novak

Agnew: the President's comment

President Nixon now has edged a bit off the sidelines in the battle within his own administration over the investigation of Vice-President Agnew. At his press conference yesterday, the President spoke with calculated vagueness. But he succeeded in leaving the impression that, despite Agnew's presumed innocence and his right to stay in office even if indicted, the President himself is not in his Vice-President's corner.

First, Mr Nixon stood firmly behind his Justice Department in rejecting Agnew's furious charges of 'malicious and outrageous' news leaks. The President said he certainly would not remove Assistant Attorney General Henry E. Petersen, chief of criminal investigations at Justice and special object of Agnew's wrath. In the Nixon book, the news leaks about the Grand Jury investigation into alleged criminal misconduct of Agnew are 'totally inexcusable and inappropriate', but the Vice-President has yet to show that they come from justice.

Second, the President refused to dismiss the charges lightly – despite Agnew's denials to him on three separate occasions that they are true. Here again, Mr Nixon's concern was the leak of the charges, while acknowledging that they are 'serious and not frivolous'.

Of course, Mr Nixon is right in pleading that Agnew should not be judged in advance on television and in the press. But Mr Nixon's own words only compound his Vice-President's troubles. The image of uncertainty surrounding Agnew is added to. The President may say that he respects the right of the Vice-President, also elected by 'all the people' to decide whether to stay in office. But Mr Nixon, who chose Agnew and has the power to make his position untenable, can hardly expect the public to believe the President is no more his Vice-President's keeper than the ordinary citizen.

In any event, Mr Nixon was not totally candid yesterday. A larger cloud than ever hangs now over the Vice-President. Neither for Agnew's own sake, nor for the sake of this already battered republic, should it be allowed to linger. Today we believe more strongly than ever in the case for a full and speedy investigation by the House of Representatives – which Agnew himself has requested and which should provide the public and Congress with the facts of his guilt or innocence.

Editorial Comment
The *Washington Post*

A vindication scenario for Agnew

There was a wonderful article published a couple of years ago in Esquire by Garry Wills describing the events that, 21 years ago, preceded the Checkers Speech. In it Mr. Wills traced (he has, alas, like Andrew Kopkind, lost the art since his total ideologization) the extraordinary political skills of the young candidate for the Vice-Presidency, Richard Nixon, who transformed a slur on his record into a triumphant public vindication and, in the course of his experience, fired a shot over the bow of Presidential candidate Dwight Eisenhower which that practiced soldier did not misinterpret.

When Eishenhower welcomed Nixon back on to the ticket as a candidate in good standing it was both because Eisenhower desired to do so, and because he was afraid not to do so.

It was then that the vindicated Mr Nixon began his celebrated Clean as a Hound's Tooth Club, and his friends and associates for many years carried about membership cards in their wallets. The resentment over Eisenhower's fitful backing never entirely dissipated, and one wonders whether Mr Agnew, in his current plight, ponders Mr Nixon's bitterness of yesteryear, and sympathizes with it.

Let's face it, guilt in the political world is not really the same thing as judicial guilt. Thomas Eagleton was not legally guilty of anything, but he was kicked off Sen. McGovern's ticket for the 'guilt' of not having divulged his record of nervous troubles to McGovern's managers. Sherman Adams was not guilty of anything much more serious than double parking, but as caught in the time-frame of the day, he was guilty, and accordingly he was dismissed.

Mr Nixon's almost truculent defense of John Ehrlichman and Bob Haldeman is in sharp contrast with the formalistic defense of Mr Agnew, and accordingly everyone rushes to the conclusion that Mr Agnew is at least politically guilty. The rumors that Mr Agnew will resign are unlikely to have originated other than from sources very close to Mr Nixon.

Let's face it, if Mr Agnew should indeed proceed to resign, Mr Nixon could hardly be sorry. For one thing there would be a purgative feel around the White House from which he himself would benefit. For another, the most conspicuous conservative-hard-liner in the United States would be neatly removed, without offending the conservative constituency that insisted on his renomination in 1972. For still another, Mr Nixon could move in someone appealing to many of his critics, thus strengthening his own embattled position.

But it is at this point that one needs to reflect on the strengths of Mr Agnew, and they are (a) institutional and, (b) personal. As regards the latter, Mr Agnew is a man of some backbone and has at least the normal man's indisposition to be pushed around. As regards the former, the Vice-President cannot be forced to resign by a show of displeasure from the President.

One hopes their personal relationship will not so deteriorate, but one could easily conceive of a situation in which the Vice-President informed the President through the press that peccadilloes allegedly committed while Governor of Maryland are surely less disqualifying than those allegedly committed while President of the United States.

If Mr Agnew is indicted, it should be recalled that every time a jury brings in a verdict of not guilty, there was an indictment that preceded it. The House might then proceed to vote impeachment, and the Senate to suspend action on the House's motion pending the trial.

If the jury then found Mr Agnew guilty, the Senate might vote accordingly. If it found him not guilty, the Senate would presumably confirm the verdict, and Mr Agnew, never having resigned the Vice-Presidency, could reoccupy the position with that distinctive strength that comes from having survived adversity.

The contrast would be damaging to President Nixon, as Garry Wills would have noticed, in days gone by.

William F. Buckley Jr.

A bitter family dispute

The controversy within the Nixon administration over Vice-President Agnew is getting sillier by the day, and the courts, which are supposed to impose reason on silliness, seem to be compounding the confusion.

Consider the facts: President Nixon is in charge of the executive branch of the Government. His principal assistant, Agnew, is informed by the President's own Attorney General that Agnew is being investigated on charges of extortion, conspiracy, tax evasion, and other felonies, and these charges are now being presented to a Federal Grand Jury in Baltimore.

And this is made public – the source of the information is still obscure – but the Vice-President announces that he is innocent, that he will not resign even if indicted, that he is the victim of a 'malicious, immoral, and illegal' attack against him by prosecutors of his own administration, and he puts the finger on Henry Petersen, head of the Criminal Division at Justice, as the source of the leaks.

So what does the President do about this public row within his own official family? He doesn't settle it but confuses it. He supports the Vice-President's right to the presumption of innocence. He says it is 'altogether right' for the Vice-President to stay in his job, even if indicted, but he adds that he has no 'clear evidence' that Asst. Atty. Gen. Petersen was responsible for the leaks or the 'malicious, immoral, and illegal' anti-Agnew attacks attributed by the Vice-President to Petersen.

Enter now the courts. Either the Vice-President's charges against Petersen were inaccurate and unfair or leaked by somebody else; or Petersen's denials, backed by Atty. Gen. Richardson were false. But in either event, this was a controversy within the administration which the President had the power to resolve – unless you assume that both Agnew and the Justice Department are now beyond his control, which may be true.

Not being resolved within the executive branch, however, the issue was left to the judiciary, and Federal District Judge Walter E. Hoffman has now ruled that Agnew's attorneys, with the full power of subpoena, may command testimony under oath about who within the Nixon administration is responsible for leaking information detrimental to their own colleague.

This raises some staggering questions for an administration that is trying to get all these Watergate and constitutional questions behind them so that they can concentrate on the 'public's business.' Are we now going to move from the Ervin Committee's interrogation of the Watergate and the 'dirty tricks' of the 1972 Presidential election to an interrogation by Agnew or his lawyers of his own colleagues in the Justice Department?

Is Petersen or even Richardson to be put on the stand under oath to swear that they didn't try to destroy their own Vice-President? And what about members of the White House staff, some of whom have also been suspected of leaking the charges against Agnew?

There must be some better way to resolve the Vice-President's suspicions. After all, this is not a conflict between political enemies. The President says he accepts the Vice-President's proclamation of innocence to the charges of political corruption, and has appealed to the nation to do the same. Meanwhile, he has stated that he has never asked the Vice-President to resign, and has not even thought about replacing him.

The later seems a little odd, but the family feud goes on, and perpetuates the doubts about the integrity of the American political system, which the President proclaims he is trying to remove.

Already, the nation is involved in more than a dozen investigations, court case, Grand Jury investigations and inter-party squabbles, all of them unavoidable on the evidence, so who needs splashy new avoidable rows with the administration itself?

The problem for the moment seems to be that everybody is looking out for his own hide, and seems willing to leave the country in a scrape rather than to risk any chance of being in a scrape himself.

So far there is no evidence that the President has even asked Agnew, Richardson and Petersen over to the White House for a quiet private talk together about their family argument.

James Reston

Petersen and the leaks

The Deputy Attorney General of the United States, William Ruckelshaus, called the other day to tell me how wrong I was to accuse his associate, Henry Petersen, of personally leaking a prejudgment of the Agnew case: 'We've got the evidence,' Peterson was quoted as saying, 'We've got it cold.'

Ruckelshaus, who has earned a reputation for being a straight shooter, said that the leak was attributed to 'sources close to the investigation,' and not Petersen himself, which the reporter has verified. My apologies: Petersen did not plant the story personally.

Then the Deputy Attorney General went on to make three points that say a great deal about the way the Agnew investigation is being conducted:

1. Petersen never said those words. Neither Petersen nor Atty. Gen. Richardson, who was in the room, remember Petersen saying that. The quote is probably a phony, they indicate now, about two weeks after the damaging pronouncement has had the widest circulation.
2. Maybe the leak came from Agnew's lawyers. Ruckelshaus was careful not to make this charge directly, but he asked rhetorically, 'Who stands to gain the most? The prosecution stands to lose if the process is poisoned by prejudicial publicity.' On this theory, the Agnew lawyers would be willing to blacken the name of their client and help speed his indictment, in order to

win on appeal. It seems far-fetched: The three Agnew attorneys have offered to swear to the contrary and Ruckelshaus wisely backed off it.

3. 'Petersen probably did use some strong language along those lines to attorneys for other potential defendants.' With that, Ruckelshaus went to the heart of the matter.

Put yourself in Henry Petersen's shoes: You have been made to look like a bumbling cover-upper before the Watergate Committee. Your lifelong reputation as a tough cop has been unfairly compromised. Your old boss, John Mitchell, is testifying that there were illegalities connected with the extension of FBI wiretaps, which could point right at you as a cornercutter. And a major Justice Department scandal is about to break which will reveal that you and an associate improperly signed somebody else's name to 'notifications' of the right to wiretap which could result in 159 criminal cases being thrown out by the Supreme Court.

In those circumstances, you have a natural desire to be known as the First Prosecutor To Get A Vice-President. This will bring you immunity from criticism from anti-Agnew mouth-pieces who believe that civil liberties do not exist for anybody to the right of Daniel Ellsberg.

Accordingly, you call in a series of attorneys for a group of scared, and possibly guilty, men. You say, in effect, that the first one in gets the best deal. (You might have even used that phrase, but I am reluctant to use direct quotes from recounted conversations.)

You proceed to blackjack them: if their clients don't talk, or if they do not say the right thing when they do talk, they go to jail. But if they do say what the prosecutor wants to hear, they go scot free: This is not called bribery and coercion, the euphemism is 'immunity,' and it powerfully concentrates the mind.

In the course of these blackjacking, Petersen says – repeatedly – that he already has an airtight case against the Vice-President. He spreads the word far and wide, to dozens of attorneys whose clients' interests calls for its leakage, that the head of the Criminal Division of the Department of Justice has the evidence 'cold' to convict the Vice-President.

Then Henry Petersen turns to Elliot Richardson and William Ruckelshaus and says – Leak? Who, me? I never talked to a reporter. Where could this terrible prejudicial publicity be coming from?

'The average citizen does not know how the immunity statues can be abused,' says the Vice-President. 'When some guy sees a jail cell opening up, and a prosecutor says to him, 'Wait – you don't have to go, just tell us about Mandel, or Agnew' – do you have any idea what that does to the system of justice?'

Every one of the lawyers who were the target of the arm-twisting by Henry Petersen should be given the opportunity, under oath and with no prejudice to their clients, to report exactly what blackjacking they were subjected to.

Is it proper for the head of the Criminal Investigation Division of the Department of Justice to broadcast his assessment of any man's guilt in a series of meetings? Ruckelshaus won't say – but the Petersen technique of guilt-by-pronouncement makes a mockery of the assurance given to the President that Petersen was 'in no way involved' with leaks or otherwise 'guilty of an indiscretion.'

William Safire

The Press and the Agnew case

The current administration has a genius for pushing the country into situations which place undue and unwelcome stress on our durable old Constitution. The latest in the line of a seemingly unending stream of sharp constitutional tests has been posed by Vice-President Agnew's assertion that the Department of Justice has engaged in a systematic and deliberate campaign of leaking information to the press in an effort to destroy him politically, in the course of destroying any chance he may have of receiving a fair hearing before a grand or petite jury. This has led to issuance by Mr Agnew's lawyers of subpoenas to reporters from the *Washington Post*, the *Washington Star News*, the *New York Times*, the *New York Daily News*, CBS News, NBC News, and *Newsweek* and *Time* magazines. All of this presages a monumental and, in our view, an entirely avoidable constitutional confrontation over the First Amendment.

Mr Agnew revealed on Aug. 6 that he had been informed that he was the target of a Federal Grand Jury investigation. There can be no doubt that since that time numerous stories based on information from sources close to the investigation have appeared concerning the nature of the charges being made against the Vice-President, the names of the witnesses against him, his state of mind and the nature of the negotiations between his lawyers and the Department of Justice. From this, his lawyers have drawn the conclusion that 'a number of officials in the prosecutorial arm of our Government have misused their offices in an immoral and illegal attempt to drive the Vice-President from the office to which he was elected, and to assure his conviction'.

Since Judge Walter E. Hoffman issued no opinion on the motion in which this argument was made, one cannot know with certainty just how he reacted to that rather startling assertion. He gave two pretty clear indications of his thinking, however. First, he granted the Vice-President's lawyers extraordinary authority to take depositions in a criminal proceeding prior to the conclusion of Grand Jury deliberations and he gave them subpoena power to make the taking of those depositions possible. The second hint came in his very strong admonition to the Grand Jury to consider only the evidence presented to it and to disregard press reports in the case. In the course of that statement, Judge Hoffman went on to say:

> We are rapidly approaching the day when the perpetual conflict between the news media, operating as they do under freedom of speech and freedom of the press and the judicial system, charged with protecting the rights of persons under investigation for criminal acts must be resolved.

The first question is whether such a conflict really does exist. And the next question is whether this case offers the best occasion for resolving it. We believe that the answer to both questions is no. The Constitution is full of useful ambiguity which through our history has permitted reasonable men to reconcile conflicting rights and interests in a spirit of accommodation which preserves the essence of the Constitution without placing unbearable stress on our nation's institutions. Constitutional clashes have generally been avoided, and wisely so, whenever possible. Such a clash could have been avoided here.

Mr Agnew's argument is that he should not be indicted because, among other things, the prosecutors have fatally flawed their case by filling news pages and the airwaves with prejudicial information against him. While he has every right to assert that claim, we would doubt that it has much substance. The fact that the trials of Sirhan Sirhan, Angela Davis, Jack Ruby and Bobby Seale were successfully concluded indicates that American judges know very well how to pick juries in highly publicized criminal cases and we do not see how Mr Agnew's trial – if it ever comes to that – would be all that much more vulnerable to prejudicial pre-trial publicity, especially since the publicity has clearly cut both ways.

At the most, his assertions, if supported by the facts, might indicate that other prosecutors or another special prosecutor should be named to handle his case.

And that is the heart of the matter. Mr Agnew's grievance is with the Department of Justice and not – as he himself has acknowledged – with the press. The press is peripheral to his argument. Attorney General Elliot L. Richardson has conducted an investigation into the leaks alleged to have come from his department. Mr Agnew's lawyers can – as they may well have already done – subpoena the Attorney General and any officials working for him, including the FBI agents who have questioned Federal prosecutors. It is hard to believe that Mr Agnew's highly skilled defense team, building upon the information already developed within the department, cannot ferret out the information they need by means of interrogations conducted under oath.

To go beyond that by asking reporters to reveal the names of sources who gave information under a pledge of confidentiality is to jeopardize an extraordinarily important constitutional principle by use of a legal ploy that is not only premature but probably marginal in the case at hand. The First Amendment right of freedom of the press is not a right flowing to newsmen individually or collectively. It is, rather, grounded on the founding fathers' belief that only a people free to receive the greatest possible flow of information could govern themselves wisely. Thus, the right put into jeopardy here is the reader's right or the viewer's right to receive as much information as newsmen – by the exercise of their best judgment rather than that of some governmental instrumentality – can conscientiously gather and responsibly present to them.

The Agnew case illustrates the point. The professional obligation of the press is to question the veracity and probable accuracy of the information their sources have revealed. And a further mission of the press is to provide the public with as much information as possible about the fitness of elected officers to conduct the people's business; this is fundamental to public participation in the democratic process.

The ability to assure confidentiality to sources are vitally important to this mission. That ability was severely jeopardized in Branzburg v. Hayes, in which the Supreme Court decided that pledges of secrecy made by reporters did not outweigh the obligation to respond to a Grand Jury subpoena and to answer questions in a criminal investigation. If the press' ability to guarantee confidentiality is limited even more, the capacity to inform the public will be severely, if not irreparably, impaired.

This newspaper has long believed that the words of the First Amendment were sufficient unto themselves and that judicial or legislative efforts to define or codify these freedoms in precise and detailed terms are potentially damaging to the freest possible flow of information to the public. For years prior to the Branzburg decision, informal accommodations which served the interests of justice and preserved the principle of freedom of the press were possible. With the Branzburg decision on the books, each new situation presents yet another threat to the free functioning of the press. Lawyers like to say that hard cases make bad law. It can likewise be said that incautious challenges to broad constitutional principles can lead, not to greater clarity and precision, but to bad constitutional precedents – to the progressive erosion, in short, of fundamental rights which, by their very sweep and breadth, have served us well for almost two centuries.

Editorial Comment
The *Washington Post*

Four friends from the old days

I.H. (Bud) Hammerman knew Spiro T. Agnew in the sixth grade. J. Walter Jones introduced him to golf. Harry. A. Dundore Sr. hunted and fished with him. George White was his personal lawyer.

These four men have formed the Agnew inner circle for years, since before their politically mobile associate made himself well known in the state of Maryland, let alone the nation. They remain the closest of his old friends, closer than the many new ones he has acquired since becoming Vice-President of the United States.

Hammerman and Jones have been notified that they are under investigation by the same Federal Grand Jury in Baltimore that is looking into allegations of Government corruption involving Agnew. Hammerman has been reportedly seeking to co-operate with the Federal prosecutors in exchange for immunity from prosecution or for some other special consideration.

Dundore has been questioned by Federal investigators on the same matter, according to informed sources. White's name has not been mentioned in connection with the investigation.

The implication of Hammerman and Jones in the investigation – which already has resulted in the indictment of Dale Anderson, who succeeded Agnew as Baltimore County Executive in 1967 after Agnew was elected Governor – has come as a shock to many in Maryland's overlapping business and political circles.

'When I heard they were looking into Buddy Hammerman and that he was dealing for immunity, I knew that was the ball game,' one highly placed Maryland Republican said. 'Obviously they have something.'

Unlike some of their democratic counterparts in Maryland, notably the well-heeled money-raising intimates of Gov. Marvin Mandel, Hammerman and Jones are not widely known in the state or in their own party.

Hammerman, 53, is probably the better known because he is a mortgage banker, a man who finds money for real estate and other ventures, with a national reputation for being shrewd and able in this field.

His company, the S.L. Hammerman Organization Inc., of which he is the President and Chairman of the board, was started by his father. It now sells millions of dollars worth of real estate in the Baltimore area every year. The father, Sam Hammerman, who began his working life as a bricklayer, was active in Baltimore civic affairs for many years, and his son has followed in his footsteps.

Both Hammermans have headed Baltimore's Advertising Club, a lunch-and-good-causes organization of businessmen that hasn't much to do with advertising.

'Bud' Hammerman is a trim, athletic-looking man, who lives in Pikesville just outside the Baltimore city line. He is married, has four children, and belongs to the Suburban Club – an exclusive country club of mostly Jewish members.

'The Hammermans are members of Baltimore's Jewish elite. They are the city's real aristocracy in the very best sense,' said a Democratic politician who knows the family. 'Almost anything worthwhile that gets done around here gets done because Bud and people like him backed it.'

Three years ago, the American Cancer Society gave $100-a-plate testimonial dinner for Hammerman in recognition of his efforts on behalf of the charity. Both Agnew and Mandel attended.

Like many Baltimoreans with money – and some without – Hammerman has dabbled in horse racing. He has owned several horses in partnership with William J. Muth, an Army acquaintance of his who is a Baltimore public relations man with broad contacts in the Baltimore and Baltimore County business communities.

'I'd give up my religion before I'd believe Bud's done anything wrong,' Muth said recently. 'Nobody's ever gong to convince me about Bud Hammerman.'

Others aren't quite so friendly. Hammerman serves as one of the directors of the Maryland State Fair and Agricultural Society, a private group that operates the state fair and half-mile racetrack at Timonium in Baltimore County.

'He could be damn tough and persistent about pushing his ideas,' said one of the other directors. 'I tell you, it bothered a lot of us having him and Fornoff stay on the board after all this stuff broke open. I don't like it at all.'

(William Fornoff, another member of the fair's board of directors, was the top administrative assistant to both Agnew and Anderson in Baltimore County when they were the elected heads of the local government. He testified freely before the Federal Grand Jury in Baltimore, and his testimony is believed to have been instrumental in the indictment of Anderson on 39 counts involving bribery and extortion charges. Fornoff himself pleaded guilty to a minor tax charge).

Hammerman was the chairman of Agnew's 1966 gubernatorial campaign, in which Agnew won a surprise victory after the Democrats, in a bloody four-way primary, nominated a weak state-wide candidate, George Mahoney.

In 1968, indulging what has been a continuing fancy for jetting off to far places for tropical vacations, Agnew went with Hammerman for a 10-day stay at the Sheraton-Kauai Hotel in Hawaii. Hammerman had been a mortgage consultant to the Sheraton chain and arranged financing for the hotel. The chain paid Agnew's plane fare and that of his wife, as well as part of their expenses.

J. Walter Jones in the opinion of some Maryland Republicans, may be closer to the Vice-President than Hammerman. He is also even more elusive.

'It used to be you could call Walter Jones upon the telephone like a normal person,' said one Maryland legislator, a Republican. 'Now you have to go through the marine operator and try and get him on his boat, if you can get him at all. He stays pretty well hidden.'

Jones is 50. He has known Agnew for about 20 years, and has stayed close to him since – smotheringly, coattail-clutchingly close, in the opinion of some of Agnew's less intimate friends.

It was Jones who, in Agnew's early days as County Executive, persuaded him to take up golf – a game he has since continued to play, with gusto if not finesse, in company with Bob Hope, Frank Sinatra and others.

Jones's considerable fortune rests primarily on real estate, though he was also a founder of the Chesapeake National Bank, a Towson institution that has flourished over the years.

His real estate firm is J. Walter Jones & Co. It was doing a good business in the 1950s, but it was in the 1960s, with a little help from Agnew, that the firm's value soared.

Jones and some associates bought a 205-acre tract of land in Baltimore County just west of Interstate 83 in 1959. The land was rezoned for industrial use; the Baltimore County Board of Zoning Appeals, upon which Agnew then served, upheld the rezoning. Three years later, the Jones group sold 40 acres of the land for more than $10,000 an acre – four times what they had paid for it – for an industrial park.

In subsequent years, Jones became a major political fundraiser for Agnew, as well as a contributor in his own right.

In 1965, the year before Agnew was elected Governor, Agnew, Jones, Dundore and six others bought 107 acres of land in Anne Arundel County near the projected second Bay Bridge site.

Agnew and Jones sold their shares of the property after their ownership of it became public knowledge and accusations of conflict of interest were made. At the time, Agnew said, somewhat indignantly, that because he bought the land in another county from the one in which he served as County Executive, and before he became a candidate for Governor, no conflict of interest existed.

Agnew also bought stock in Jones Chesapeake National Bank and served as a director there.

Jones has been described by one Maryland Republican as 'a flamboyant, white-loafer type,' but his life of late has been one of private affluence rather than public pretension. He lives with his second wife on an estate near Annapolis now, where he maintains a yacht and according to some accounts, a magnificent wine cellar.

He has publicly acknowledged that he is under investigation by the Grand Jury in connection with alleged kickbacks to public officials – including Agnew – from engineering contractors.

Jones has firmly denied that he has done anything illegal and has defended the Vice-President with equal vigor. 'I am not aware of any kickbacks on the part of the Vice-President,' Jones said in a prepared statement issued last August when news of the investigation first broke. 'He just isn't that type of man.'

Peter A. Jay

New challenge to press freedom

With the subpoenaing of newsmen connected to the criminal investigation into the activities of Vice-President Agnew, we are headed toward a new and possibly climactic constitutional confrontation over the issue of the freedom of the press. Things at this stage don't look too promising for the media.

The newsmen involved are those who have written stories about charges being brought against Agnew and the evidence against him that is in the process of being presented to the Grand Jury in Baltimore, attributed to 'Justice Department sources.' Lawyers for the Vice-President have more than a passing interest in finding out just who these sources are. Agnew himself has charged that he has been the victim of a deliberate and calculated campaign of news leaks designed to force him out of office.

Federal Judge Walter E. Hoffman, in giving the lawyers the go-ahead to issue the subpoenas, stated the problem succinctly:

'We are rapidly approaching the day,' he said, 'when the perpetual conflict between the news media, operating as they do under freedom of speech and freedom of the press, and the judicial system charged with protecting the rights of persons under investigation for criminal acts, must be resolved.'

Newsmen, being what they are, are likely to be uncooperative in supplying the attorneys and the Grand Jury with the names of their informants. The courts, being what they are, are likely to find reporters in contempt. Some of them, quiet possibly, may wind up in jail.

In fact, the issue described by Judge Hoffman was pretty well resolved in June last year in the case of the United States against *New York Times* reporter Earl Caldwell. Caldwell had refused to disclose his sources to a Grand Jury in California investigation the Black Panthers. In that case, the Supreme Court held that there is no first amendment privilege to newsmen to refuse to answer questions of a Grand Jury, even if those questions require the disclosure of confidential sources and information.

This case is a good deal trickier – and also quite probably a good deal stickier – from the point of view of the newsmen involved. For it is not, as Judge Hoffman suggests a simple confrontation between the courts and the press.

In this case it is the Grand Jury system itself that is directly threatened by the leaks of information that is supposed to be held in strictest secrecy. And many people, including Government officials, Grand Jury witnesses and attorneys – as well as the press – are apparently conspiring to break down the secrecy without which the system cannot effectively operate.

Indeed President Nixon himself could be charged with joining in the game. He does, of course, urge that Agnew should not be 'tried and convicted in the press and on television by leaks and innuendoes'. But at the same time, he advances the judgment that the charges against the Vice-President are 'serious and not frivolous' – an opinion which in itself could affect the outcome of a Grand Jury deliberation.

The press is in an uncomfortable position in this case, lending itself to an attack on the judicial process as well as on the Vice-President – that is hard to justify as being in the public interest. Newsmen can argue that those really responsible for the leaks are the officials and others who have informed them. But then in the next breath they will insist on protecting these same informants from the retribution of the law.

Protecting sources is a religion among the news fraternity. But it is one thing to protect a source among the Black Panthers and quite another to claim a right to protect informants who are systematically engaged in subverting the judicial system itself.

It may come down in the end to the fact that the investigation of possible criminal activities of a President or Vice-President is not the same as an investigation of criminal activities by ordinary citizens. Agnew himself has suggested as much in denying the jurisdiction of the courts in his case and demanding impeachment proceedings by the House before any judicial action is taken.

This in itself is virtually the same thing as asking to be tried before the 'bar of public opinion' to determine the essential issue, with is Agnew's fitness to remain in office over the next three years. It is, in short, a political rather than a judicial matter, in the Vice-President's own view. And if this is how he prefers to be tried, then the press does indeed play an essential role in the process.

Crosby S. Noyes

A subdued Agnew praises President

Chicago – Vice-President Spiro T. Agnew abandoned his fiery denunciation of those he says are engaged in a vendetta against him in favor of a subdued – almost somber – speech here in which he effusively praised President Nixon.

Agnew was the principal speaker at a Republican fund-raising dinner here last night, only five days after a Los Angeles address in which he unleashed a fierce rhetorical attack against the Justice Department and others he claims are acting illegally in a Federal Grand Jury investigation of his activities.

The audience of more than 1,000 Illinois Republicans and the dozens of reporters on hand had expected another round of sharp criticism from Agnew, directed principally at the Government prosecutors in charge of the Baltimore probes of bribery, extortion and tax fraud allegations against Maryland businessmen and politicians, including Agnew.

The United Republican Fund of Illinois, sponsor of the dinner, had reported that ticket sales, at $125 a head, were relatively slow until a few days ago, when hundreds of reservations poured in after the California speech. And Agnew's staff had advised reporters to expect another hard-hitting speech.

But Agnew began his address with a remark directed to the reporters and couched in terms of motion picture ratings:

'This may save some overtime. Tonight is not going to be an X-rated political show. It's just going to be PG, so if you have to go somewhere, go.'

Then he added a wistful and somewhat cryptic reference: 'A candle is only so long, and eventually it burns out.'

The Vice-President then proceeded to deliver his prepared speech. The only theme was that Republicans are interested only in Federal programs which truly help the people, as contrasted to the 'eclectic scatter-gun programs' of recent Democratic administrations whose hallmark Agnew said was 'public ballyhoo' but poor results.

Robert Walters

Offers house time to act Agnew not immune, justice dept. insists

The Justice Department firmly contends Vice-President Spiro T. Agnew is not immune from criminal prosecution under the Constitution and is subject to indictment by the Federal Grand Jury investigating him in Baltimore.

The Department yesterday also expressed its intention to allow the House 'a reasonable time' to consider the 'desirability of impeachment proceedings' against Agnew if he is indicted, before bringing him to trial.

But the Department took the position that any such pause would only be in 'deference to the House' after any indictment of Agnew and is 'not constitutionally required'. It said only the President enjoys immunity from prosecution.

The Justice Department's position was laid out in a brief filed in US District Court in Baltimore yesterday in reply to the contention by lawyers for Agnew that 'the Constitution forbids that the Vice-President be indicted or tried in any criminal court.

The brief, signed by Solicitor Gen. Robert. H. Bork, acknowledged that the Vice-President's motion to enjoin the jury, now receiving evidence against him, 'poses a grave and unresolved constitutional issue'.

But it rejected Agnew's contention that he stands equal with the President under the Constitution with the same rights, protection and immunity.

The Government said no immunity exists for the Vice-President 'where none is mentioned.'

Ronald Sarro

Jury probes Agnew home purchase

The Federal Grand Jury investigating Vice-President Spiro T. Agnew has subpoenaed records relating to the Agnews' purchase of their $190,000 home in suburban Maryland, according to the real estate agent who handled the transaction.

Peter Burr, the realtor, also said yesterday that he did not receive any commission for negotiating the Agnews' house purchase, and thereby reduced the price they paid by $4,000 to $6,000.

Vice-President and Mrs. Agnew bought the 12-room fieldstone house in the fashionable Kenwood area of Montgomery county with the help of a $160,000 mortgage obtained from the American National Building and Loan Association of Baltimore.

According to land records the Agnews made a $30,000 down payment for the house at 6415 Shadow Rd., where they moved in June from their apartment at the Sheraton-Park Hotel in Washington.

Records relating to the Agnews' mortgage apparently have been subpoenaed from American National. Howard I. Scaggs, President of the Building and Loan Association, declined yesterday to either confirm or deny this.

Burr, a partner in the real estate firm of Burr, Morris and Pardoe, said that his records of the Agnews' purchase were subpoenaed on Sept. 25 by the Baltimore Grand Jury investigating allegations of kickbacks to public officials, including Agnew.

Burr said that he gave up the usual 2 to 3 per cent commission for selling the house to the Agnews when it became clear that the Agnews and the seller, Dorothy Bennett and partner, might not otherwise be able to agree on a price. Burr also said he was given written assurance that he will handle sale of the house at any time the Agnews want to sell.

The Agnews' mortgage amounts to about eighty-five percent of the house's $190,000 purchase price. Scaggs said that because of the size of the loan, the Agnews also pledged as security in addition to the Kenwood house, a Baltimore County house valued at $25,000 that the Vice-President inherited from his parents.

Local savings and loan officials said yesterday that presently few home purchasers could get a mortgage for more than 75 to 80 per cent of a home's sale price, although money was less tight when the Agnews bought their home last spring.

Scaggs said the $160,000 mortgage loan to the Agnews was in line with the total of $215,000 in real estate they pledged as security and they did not benefit from any special favoritism on the mortgage. He said the Agnews' mortgage is not the largest approved by American National.

The Agnews are required to make monthly mortgage payments of $1,118.72.

'They make monthly payments just like anyone else,' said Scaggs.

Since August, the Federal Grand Jury in Baltimore has subpoenaed many of Agnew's financial records in connection with its investigation of the Vice-President on alleged bribery, extortion, conspiracy and tax charges.

Agnew has repeatedly declared his innocence of the charges. He recently moved to block the Grand Jury investigation on constitutional grounds and because of his contention that leaks to the press have made it impossible for him to obtain a fair hearing.

Douglas Watson

With Agnew, duty first

Once in the hills, a long time ago, I heard the cry of a trapped fox – a cry of pure pain, coupled with wild anger and resentment. There was a poignant echo of that cry in Vice-President Agnew's speech to the Republican women last weekend.

I have such sympathy for the poor devil, and such contempt for the faceless 'sources' who have trapped him, that it is difficult to write dispassionately of his plight. Yet he is, after all, Vice-President of the United States. He is one heartbeat removed from the most powerful office in the free world, and his extraordinary statement has to be quietly examined.

'I will not resign if indicted.' This was his pledge and in the steamy emotionalism of the hour, it is understandable that his partisan audience cheered him to the rafters. Yet it is a pledge that, in the event, Agnew will have to reconsider. His first duty as he himself clearly understands, is to the unique office he holds; and a keen sense of that duty in the end will govern his decision.

Under the Constitution, a Vice-President has but one official duty: he is to preside over the Senate and cast a tie-breaking vote if the chamber is evenly divided. His infinitely greater duty, of course, is simply to stand by, and to keep himself prepared in every possible way for the moment when the heartbeat stops.

Those born in this century have known four such moments: September 14, 1901, when McKinley died of wounds suffered a week earlier; August 2, 1923; when Harding died in San Francisco; April 12, 1945, when Roosevelt succumbed to a stroke in Warm Springs; and November 22, 1963, when Kennedy fell to an assassin's bullet.

It is not morbid speculation – it is simple prudence – to recognize that such a moment could come again at any time. At 60, Richard Nixon appears in excellent health; he is surrounded by every conceivable safeguard against accidental death or assassination; but Nixon is as mortal as other men, and he is the object, as every President must be, of fanatical hatred. We have to suppose the tragic moment may arrive.

Agnew must ask himself if the shaken country, in such an event, could effectively be governed by a President under criminal indictment for bribery, tax evasion and kickbacks. It is a terrible question to ask, but Agnew's own speech compels its public examination; the question, in my own view, answers itself: The Vice-President, if indeed he is indicted, would have to resign. His own understanding of his standby duty would leave him no other course.

In his Los Angeles speech, Agnew lunged in anger – justifiable anger – against his tormentors within the Justice Department. The persons responsible for the leaks to the press in recent months deserve all the condemnation he heaped upon them. These sources presumably are lawyers, officers of the court, men bound by honor and tradition to respect the rights of an accused. They have behaved outrageously.

At the same time, it is regrettable that the Vice-President moved beyond these malicious gossips in order to attack the whole system of criminal justice. To describe this system as 'poison,' and to insist that he could not obtain a fair trial, is to impugn the Baltimore District Court without cause. Judge Walter Hoffman of Norfolk, who is presiding there by designation, is an experienced jurist, highly regarded by observers who have watched him grow on the bench. If the Grand Jury indicts, Agnew would be assured his fair day in court.

Like the trapped fox, the Vice-President is already badly hurt. But the fox pulled himself free; he survived; he nursed his mangled paw and went on about his business. Agnew has the same valiant spirit. He may yet limp away from this agonizing experience, wounded but triumphant, capable of running in the political hills again.

James J. Kilpatrick

The fate of other vice-presidents under fire

Vice-President Agnew, in asking the House of Representatives to make a 'full inquiry' into charges against him, cited as a precedent the case of Vice-President Calhoun. The case of two other Vice-Presidents also are being recalled.

John C. Calhoun was Vice-President, 1825–32, under Presidents John Quincy Adams and Andrew Jackson. He was accused in a Virginia newspaper in 1826 of irregularities when he had served as Secretary of War in a previous Administration. There was no official charge, no Grand Jury investigation. The accusation was that Mr Calhoun had profiteered from a War department contract for building a fort.

Mr Calhoun asked the House of Representatives to investigate the matter. The Speaker put the request before the House. It was referred to a select committee of seven members, which permitted the Vice-President to be represented by counsel and have the right to compel testimony.

Early in 1827, the committee majority submitted its report. It concluded that Mr Calhoun had not personally benefited from the contract. It proposed that no further action be taken by the House. The matter was dropped.

Schuyler Colfax, who served 1869–73 under President Ulysses S. Grant, was named in the report of a Congressional

Committee as one of several persons who had been given stock in Credit Mobilier, a company involved in construction of the Union Pacific railroad. Mr Colfax was alleged to have received the stock when he was Speaker of the House in 1867. The committee report, published in February, 1873, made no recommendation as to action against Vice-President Colfax. The matter was referred to the House Judiciary Committee, which, by a vote of 7 to 1, recommended against impeachment proceedings. The Judiciary Committee's report stated:

'It will readily be seen that the remedial proceedings of impeachment should only be applied to high crimes and misdemeanors committed while in office and which alone affect the officer in discharge of his duties as such, whatever may have been their effect upon him as a man, for impeachment touches the office only and qualifications for the office, and not the man himself.'

The House took no further action. Mr Colfax's term as Vice-President expired on March 4, 1873.

Aaron Burr was Vice-President under Thomas Jefferson from 1801 to 1803. In 1804, he was indicted for murder after the duel in which he killed Alexander Hamilton in July of that year.

The murder indictment was handed down by a court in Bergen County, N.J. There was talk in Congress of moving to impeach Mr Burr, but nothing came of it. History is not entirely clear on the reasons why, but it appears that President Jefferson, who controlled both the House and the Senate, was able to prevent both from acting against his Vice-President. In the Senate, in fact, a petition was circulated and signed by several members, asking the Governor of New Jersey to quash the murder indictment against Mr Burr. He was never brought to trial.

Vice-President Burr served out his term, and during this time presided over the impeachment trial of Supreme Court Justice Samuel Chase, who was found not guilty by the Senate.

Editorial Comment
The *Washington Post*

Pleads on tax evasion
Agnew resigns

Agnew Letters

Here are the texts of Spiro T. Agnew's formal letter of resignation as Vice-President, sent to Secretary of State Henry A. Kissinger under statutory procedures; Agnew's letter of resignation to President Nixon, and Nixon's reply to Agnew:

Dear Mr Secretary:

I hereby resign the office of Vice-President of the United States, effective immediately.

Sincerely
(s) Spiro T. Agnew

Dear Mr President:

As you are aware the accusations against me cannot be resolved without a long, divisive and debilitating struggle in the Congress and the courts. I have concluded that, painful as it is to me and to my family, it is in the best interests of the nation that I relinquish the Vice-Presidency.

Accordingly, I have today resigned the office of Vice-President of the United States. A copy of the instrument of resignation is enclosed.

It has been a privilege to serve with you. May I express to the American people, through you my deep gratitude for the confidence in twice electing me to be Vice-President.

Sincerely,
(s) Spiro T. Agnew

Nixon Reply

Dear Ted:

The most difficult decisions are often those that are the most personal, and I know your decision to resign as Vice-President has been as difficult as any facing a man in public life could be. Your departure from the administration leaves me with a great sense of personal loss. You have been a valued associate through these nearly five years that we have served together.

However, I respect your decision, and I also respect the concern for the national interest that led you to conclude that a resolution of the matter in this way, rather than through an extended battle in the courts and the Congress, was advisable in order to prevent a protracted period of national division and uncertainty.

As Vice-President, you have addressed the great issues of our times with courage and candor. Your strong patriotism and your profound dedication to the welfare of the nation have been an inspiration to all who have served with you as well as to millions of others throughout the country.

I have been deeply saddened by this whole course of events, and I hope that you and your family will be sustained in the days ahead by a well justified pride in all that you have contributed to the nation by your years of service as Vice-President.

Sincerely,
(s) Richard Nixon

The *Washington Post*

Agnew decision 'stunned' staff

Spiro T. Agnew's decision to leave the Vice-Presidency was kept secret from most members of his staff.

They were told at 2 PM in Agnew's offices in the Executives Office Building adjacent to the White House. 'There was dead silence,' one staff member said. 'We were all deeply moved and stunned.'

Agnew arrived for work on his last day in office shortly after 9 AM and remained in his office until about 1 PM, when he left for the US District Court in Baltimore.

According to one staff member, he had no outside callers. Instead he worked quietly with his chief of staff Arthur J. Sohmer.

According to his Agnew aide, Sohmer and Maj. Gen. John N. Dunn, who broke the news to the staff, were probably the only ones on his staff who knew of Agnew's decision.

The Agnew assistant said he was certain the Vice-President talked his decision over with his family and lawyers but apparently arrived at the decision himself. In retrospect, he said he thought the Vice-President's decision began to crystallize about the time he spoke at a convention of Republican women in Los Angeles.

In that speech on Sept 29, he angrily defended himself against the accusations of criminal wrongdoing and accused officials in the Justice Department of trying to get him as a 'trophy' for fumbling the Watergate case.

The Senate adopted a resolution yesterday extending the pay of members of former Vice-President Spiro T. Agnew's Senate staff for 30 days.

United Press International

Agnew big news around the world

The resignation of Spiro T. Agnew as Vice-President has been featured on front pages of newspapers around the world, with editorial reaction ranging from sympathetic to condemning.

The Agnew story was displayed on the front pages of all Egyptian newspapers without comment. It was virtually the only story not dealing with the Middle East war to receive front page treatment.

The Soviet press printed a brief report on the resignation, saying 'accusations were made against Agnew blaming him for taking bribes and evading paying income taxes while he was Governor of Maryland. Agnew acknowledged his guilt on one point of the accusation – evasion of income taxes.'

There was no editorial opinion.

In Greece, the country of Agnew's ancestors, the resignation made front page news in every daily paper.

In Amsterdam, the liberal paper *De Volkskrant* editorialized: 'Why should the Vice-President be singled out for an offense which can be imputed to numerous American politicians?'

One conclusion, the paper said, was that 'a scapegoat was needed to divert attention from Watergate'.

In Italy, Turin's *la Stampa* stated a similar opinion in its headline: SACRIFICED TO MAKE PEOPLE FORGET WATERGATE?

But Rotterdam's independent *Algemeen Dagblad* declared, 'The resignation of Agnew is sensible and no loss for America.'

The liberal London *Guardian* termed Agnew's resignation 'a shabby bargain.' It added, 'That by resigning he should have been able to get away with a guilty plea to a minor charge resulting in a three year probation order is not likely to inspire new confidence in American political leaders.'

Aftonbladet, a Socialist Democrat paper in Stockholm, said that while the 'perhaps slightly criminal' Vice-President has to go, 'the real leaders and criminals stay'.

In Rio de Janeiro, the *Journal do Brasil* said, 'The whole world is, for the first time, witnessing a terrible historical crisis, and the first aspect brought up in this American tragedy is the democratic courage with which it is being faced.'

Associated Press

'The man is a crook,' US attorney says

Chicago (UPI) – US Atty. James R. Thompson says he has never seen a stronger case of bribery or extortion than the one the government had developed against Spiro T. Agnew.

'The man is a crook, no question about that at all,' Thompson declared.

Thompson, US Attorney for the Northern District of Illinois, had been chosen by the Justice Department to defend the Government against Agnew's charges of prejudicial press leaks. He made the comments at a news conference on his return to Chicago yesterday.

Thompson said he thought that the solution of the case was 'on the whole a good resolution. I have no doubt that if the (former) Vice-President had stood trial and been convicted, he would have been sentenced to a very large number of years,' Thompson said.

United Press International

'And then they knifed him'
Agnew resignation evokes some bitter views

Some spoke bitterly yesterday of Spiro T. Agnew.

Elaine Tutman, a restaurant inspector in Prince George's County, called him 'a hatchet man who served Mr Nixon well' and said his resignation is 'just another example of a loyal employee being rewarded.'

'He made the speeches, called the names, and then they knifed him when they wanted to get Connally in as Vice-President,' said the 38-year old inspector, who prefers to be called Ms Tutman.

She said she believed Agnew's fall is the result of a Nixon-backed conspiracy 'that goes back to the Justice Department.' She was among persons interviewed at random yesterday at three shopping centers in suburban Maryland.

Others had a far different opinion.

Three young Forestville mothers who were shopping at Iverson Mall with their infants believe Agnew has been unfairly punished.

'There are ghosts in everyone's closet,' said Lana Sylier, 25, the wife of a DC police officer. 'Many other officeholders have done the same thing.'

'He took money. So what?' said Kathy Erdner, 22, the wife of an Air Force man stationed at Andrews Air Force Base.

Gayle Arigo, 25, agreed that Agnew is 'a nice guy. Money talks. It turns a lot of heads. They should merely have spanked his hand, told him not to do it again. But he should not have resigned. He's a character.'

Mrs Sylier said, 'Everyone cheats on their taxes. Of course I do. The Government takes so much money from you, if I can take some of it back, I will.'

Mrs Erdner wondered 'why Watergate is being exposed, after this kind of thing has been going on for centuries.'

Mrs Arigo suggested that 'if the news media had been as active in Lincoln's day, he would never have been so pontifical.'

All three women agreed they might vote for Agnew if he ran again for public office.

Majorie Waddell is 'beginning to think the country should listen more to its young people.' She said her teenage daughter is 'very concerned' and would make 'a good honest politician.'

Mrs Waddell, of 3701 Silver Park Dr., Suitland, thinks that 'two-thirds of our politicians are corrupt.' As a result, she said, 'the big guys are taking over the country. Small contractors are being pushed out. The whole mess disgusts me.'

Mrs Waddell said she supported Agnew as Governor 'and thought the world of him. He kept the DC riots from coming across the border.'

But she was concerned about his punishment. She recalled that a funeral director in her hometown in Virginia 'went to prison for six months because he failed to pay a few thousand dollars in taxes. He was a nice person but he paid. And it ruined his business and his life.'

Back in Illinois we feel as if he's let his friends down.' Ross said, 'Who else do we have to look up to if not our leaders? This whole Watergate thing has hurt the country, crippled the economy.'

Stanley Collinge, a retired professional golfer who lives at 6100 Wilmet Dr., Bethesda, thinks that 'the people who greased Agnew's palms should be prosecuted too. They're just as guilty.'

'It takes a weak man to accept a bribe,' Collinge said, 'but they benefited too.'

Helen Fox, a Silver Spring housewife, suggested to a reporter that 'if it had been you, the sentence wouldn't have been so light.'

President Nixon 'didn't need any more trouble,' she said, but now that he must choose a new Vice-President, Mrs Fox nominated Sen. Sam Ervin. 'He's real cute.'

Tom Newman, 24, a carpenter from Gaithersburg, believes Agnew 'should have gone to jail.' Newman wants the investigation to continue. He characterized Agnew as 'just another guy Nixon chose who screwed up.'

Thomas Lambert, a retired ice cream company salesman who has moved from Washington to Port Tabacco, Md., 'can't understand why we don't get some of the other crooks. Most politicians are corrupt and Maryland is the crookest state in the US. Lots more of them belong in jail.'

Although he did not defend Agnew, Lambert wondered 'why your biased paper doesn't take after some of the other bad guys – Dowdy, Brewster, (state Sen.) Mitchell.'

While he is disappointed with Agnew's actions, Lambert remains 'glad I didn't vote for that yellow-bellied McGovern.'

One of the more optimistic persons interviewed was Joan Lally of Greenbelt, who said she doesn't think 'the majority of public officials take bribes.'

But then there was Bruce Lockhart, at Chevy Chase 'All politicians are crooked. The best we can hope for is that some of them are crooked for the people.'

Donald P. Baker

Agnew departure jolts Marylanders

Marylanders, including many who campaigned for and against Spiro T. Agnew as he rose from a position on a suburban Baltimore zoning board to the Vice-Presidency of the United States, received the news of his resignation yesterday which shock, dismay and even a sense of betrayal.

In Greek neighborhoods in Baltimore where Agnew grew up there was sorrow that a man whose political successes had given old neighbors so much pride had left his high office in disgrace, accepting without contest a verdict of guilty to charges of tax evasion, a $10,000 fine and a suspended three year prison term.

Here and there across the state there was rage – not so much at Agnew as at President Nixon, whom many Marylanders saw as being in some way responsible for the plight of the Vice-President, their former Governor.

Maryland Gov. Marvin Mandel, who became Governor after Agnew was elected Vice-President, said that Agnew's decision to resign 'took courage and determination'.

Agnew, Mandel said, 'placed the stability of the nation, the integrity of the Vice-Presidency and the security of his family above a political future.'

Thomas Hunger Lowe, the former Democratic speaker of the Maryland House of delegates who was sworn in this week as a judge on the state Court of Special Appeals, said he was 'really shaken' by the news of Agnew's resignation.

'If it's true, if he took cold payoffs, it means a hell of a lot of people had a hell of a lot of misplaced faith. I would have damn near staked my life on his innocence. The comment I've heard around here (Easton, on Maryland's Eastern Shore) is that it's a shame it wasn't Nixon,' Lowe said.

'Agnew was the rock upon which this whole administration has been stabilized.'

In the Highlandtown area of Baltimore, a Greek working-class area, there was gloom. Agnew, whose immigrant father changed his name from Anagnostopoulos, is still admired by Greek-Americans, and there was resentment at his resignation.

At Spiro A's Princess Cafe, owned and operated by Spiro S. Asimenior, Spiro Agnew's predicament took conversational precedence over that of the Baltimore orioles, who at that point were trailing in their playoff game with Oakland.

'I think he was forced into it,' said proprietor Asimenior. 'The pressure of the news media and the TV convicted him before he was even charged.'

'Nixon put the pressure on him,' said Jim Sieling, a patron, as he sipped a beer. 'There was no sign of them investigating Agnew until Nixon got into trouble with Watergate. Now with Spiro in trouble, you don't even hear about Watergate.'

Sieling suggested that Agnew should run against Mandel. 'He could probably be Governor, even if he is on probation,' he said.

Maryland's two Republican US senators, J. Glenn Beall Jr. and Charles McC. Mathias, had little to say about Agnew.

Beall, whose brother, George Beall, is the US Attorney in Baltimore who headed the investigation of Agnew and other political figures, said he was 'saddened' by the resignation.

Mathias, who has frequently been at odds with Agnew and the Nixon administration, had no public comment. Some GOP congressmen, however, were not so reticent. Maryland Rep. Lawrence J. Hogan, who had supported Agnew's unsuccessful request that the House of Representatives hear his case (and thereby delay court proceedings), said he was 'stunned, dumbfounded'.

'A number of us who responded to (Agnew's) request for a House hearing are out on a limb that he's just sawed off,' Hogan said. 'But you can't blame the man. His own situation has to be paramount.'

Rep. Robert Bauman, who won an upset victory in a special election last August that he attributed in part to Agnew's campaigning on his behalf, said he was 'highly surprised. I took him at his word on his previous statements.'

Bauman noted that Agnew's plea of *nolo contendere*, or no contest, to Federal charges that he evaded payment of $13,551.47 in income taxes for 1967 (while he was Governor) was 'for all intents and purposes the same as a guilty plea.'

Reps. Gilbert Guide and Marjorie Holt, both Maryland Republicans, said they were 'shocked' at Agnew's resignation. Gov. Linwood Holton of Virginia said he was 'sorry'.

In Towson, where Agnew practiced law and served as Baltimore County Axecutive before he was elected Governor in 1966, reaction ranged from the somber to the philosophical.

Ken Smith, Agnew's barber declared that 'everyone here thinks this is just Nixon's trick to get (former Treasury Secretary John) Connally in as Vice-President.'

Lawyers in Agnew's old firm weren't talking, but William J. Bregle, the manager of a Towson men's clothing store, said he was an old Kiwansis Club friend of the Vice-President and was sure Agnew would be welcomed back.

'He's a fine man. This doesn't change my feelings about him,' Bregle said. 'It's just one of those things that crop up in political life.'

That's particularly true in Towson. Agnew's successor as County Executive, Dale Anderson, has been indicted by the same Federal Grand Jury in Baltimore on more than 40 counts of bribery, extortion and tax evasion.

Two other former Towson lawyers and public figures, former House Speaker A. Gordon Boone and former US Sen. Daniel B. Brewster, both Democrats, have been convicted of Federal crimes committed while in office. Boone served one year in jail. Brewster is still free on appeal.

Bruce Longbuttom, a Towson insurance man, said that Agnew's 'was another Horatio Alger story. He always fought for what he thought was right, and we admired that. I guess they just had the goods on him, otherwise I don't think he would have given in.'

George P. Mahoney, the perennial Democratic contender for high office in Maryland whom Agnew narrowly defeated in 1966 to become Governor, was one of the small number of people interviewed who said he wasn't surprised.

'No, it doesn't strike me as a great surprise,' said Mahoney, now the head of Maryland's Lottery Commission. 'All these things were done in our very own town and I don't accept it as a surprise.

'Why, in 1966 he called me a bigot and a racist, all those outrageous dirty tricks, none of it was true what he said about me in the campaign. It was worse than the dirty tricks used in the Watergate, and he never apologized to me after it was over.'

Other reactions varied. Leroy Busa, 48, an engineer from Springfield, Va., said he thought Agnew 'got off lightly'. He voted for the Nixon ticket in 1968 and 1972, he said, but would have 'very serious doubt' about voting for a Republican in 1976.

At Tom's Bar a Baltimore tavern, Anthony E. Gallagher said he was 'one hundred percent for Agnew'. Gallagher said he is an active Democrat, and thinks Agnew was trapped by the President. 'I think Nixon set him up,' Gallagher said. 'I think he should have fought it' and not resigned.

Peter A. Jay

Anonymous call to IRS office sparked Agnew investigation

The investigation of Vice-President Spiro T. Agnew, who pleaded no context to an income tax evasion charge after resigning yesterday, began last fall with a telephone call to the Internal Revenue Service.

The caller, a former employee of a Baltimore County engineering firm, reportedly told an IRS agent: 'If you go to Baltimore County you'll find some interesting things.'

The IRS went. The evidence it began turning over to the US Attorney's office in Baltimore resulted in the formation of a special Grand Jury there in December, 1972, to investigate corruption in sprawling Baltimore County, which all but surrounds the city.

In January Federal prosecutors hauled away a truckload of Baltimore County government records, and, as well, subpoenaed records of more than a score of consulting engineers and architects doing business with the county.

At the start of the investigation, the targets were believed to be Baltimore County's present and former Democratic officials – not Agnew. US Attorney George Beall had assured Justice Department superiors that no matter what the wide-ranging probe uncovered, it would not mean a prosecution of Agnew.

Beall pointed out that the statute of limitations for criminal offenses is five years and for tax offenses is six and Agnew had left as County Executive when elected Governor of Maryland in 1966, more than six years earlier.

But despite Beall's original prediction, the evidence broadened and reached into more recent years, when Agnew was Governor and Vice-President. Agnew's no contest plea to the tax evasion charge involved tax returns for 1967, when he was Governor.

In February of this year, Agnew later said at a press conference, friends told him there were 'rumors in the cocktail circuit that various allegations coming out of the investigation have mentioned my name'.

In April, Agnew said, a lawyer that he had hired contacted the prosecutors to tell them 'I would in no way attempt to impede the investigation'.

Agnew apparently became a definite target of the investigation sometime during the spring, after prosecutors had questioned former Baltimore County administrator William E. Fornoff and consulting engineers Jerome B. Wolff and Lester Matz.

In May, and June Wolff and Matz appeared before the investigators several times and according to sources, both hinted that in return for immunity from prosecution they would be willing to supply information on Agnew.

On June 4 Fornoff, who served immediately under Agnew when Agnew was County Executive, pleaded guilty to a minor tax charge and agreed to co-operate with the prosecutors.

On Aug. 1 Beall sent a letter to Agnew's lawyer, formally informing him that the Vice-President was under investigation for possible bribery, extortion, tax and conspiracy violations. The letter was disclosed on Aug. 6.

Two days later Agnew called a nationally televised press conference to denounce reports that he took kickbacks from contractors as 'damned lies'. Agnew added: 'I have nothing to hide.' Throughout August, the investigation of Agnew intensified. On Aug. 22 Agnew, referring to news reports of the investigation called a press conference to charge 'some Justice Department officials have decided to indict me in the press' and to again declare his innocence of any wrongdoing.

On Aug. 23 Baltimore County Executives Dale Anderson, Agnew's successor and a Democrat, was indicted on 39 counts involving bribery and extortion. On Sept 18 the *Washington Post* reported that Agnew recently had held long discussions with friends about the advisability of his resignation and that one Republican party leader who met with Agnew came away convinced Agnew would shortly give up his office.

Later, Agnew's attorneys were reported to be plea bargaining on the Vice-President's behalf.

On Sept 25 Attorney General Elliot L. Richardson announced that the prosecutors would present their case against Agnew to the Grand Jury. Agnew immediately called on the House of Representatives to investigate him instead. The House leadership refused. On Sept. 28 Agnew's attorneys, contending that the Constitution shields the Vice-President from prosecution, asked the court to halt the Grand Jury investigation.

The next day Agnew said in a nationally televised California speech, 'I will not resign if indicated'. Agnew attacked Justice Department officials for considering him a 'big trophy', denied he had been plea bargaining and told a warmly applauding crowd: 'I want to say at this point clearly and unequivocally: I am innocent of the charges against me.'

Douglas Watson

Resignation draws a mixed reaction

'I'm a little ashamed,' said Jean Armour upon learning of the resignation of Vice-President Spiro T. Agnew.

'As Americans, I guess we must accept part of the responsibility when this happens to one of our elected officials,' said Mrs Armour, an Oakton housewife who learned the news about 4:45 PM upon emerging from a matinee performance at the National Theater here.

A group of senior English students from Crossland High School in Prince George's County, who attended the same show, placed most of the blame for the move by their state's former Governor on President Nixon.

'I'm not surprised,' said Bill Triplett, one of the students. 'It was obvious that Agnew was being played as a diversionary tactic by Nixon. Sooner or later he (Agnew) would be found guilty.'

'Nixon pushed it – through leaks from Justice,' added Glen Barrentine. 'It's wonderful,' shouted Jason Janowiak. 'I knew anyone connected with Nixon couldn't be all good.'

Classmate Laura Nunemaker was 'shocked,' however, because 'Agnew said he wouldn't resign.' Susan Valenta came as close to having a kind word as was offered by the students. 'It may be true,' she said, 'but we shouldn't forget that Nixon has done a lot of good.'

Delores Washington, a Government Services Industry employee, said she believes Agnew 'should have done it a long time ago.'

'And Tricky Dick with him,' chimed in W.E. Pinson, a DC schools employee who was in the same bus queue at 10th Pennsylvania Avenue NW.

'Right on,' responded Miss Washington.

Victor Stagnaro, a vacationer from San Mateo, Calif., agreed with his wife, who said, 'We've lost track of all this for a while. That's why a vacation is so good for you.'

A man paused in the National Press Building lobby to buy cigarettes, heard a radio report of the resignation and said aloud, 'Beautiful.' The announcer then reported that the New York Mets had won the National League pennant, and the man added, 'It's a beautiful day all around.'

Sterling Levie, who works for the Maryland Highway Administration in Hagerstown, was disappointed that Agnew 'didn't go through and fight it.' Levi told a friend, Randolph Hein, a sheet metal worker from Hartland, Wis., that 'kickbacks have been a custom in Maryland for years.'

Hein said 'I think both of them should be taken out.'

Gene Calir, of Boston, who voted for Nixon last year as 'the lesser of two evils.' said 'you can lay a lot of the blame at the doorstep of Richard Nixon. I'm disappointed in a system that lets this go on. But nothing excuses malfeasance or misfeasance.'

Toni Kress, a lobby bartender at the Statler Hilton Hotel, squealed, 'He did? Good,' upon hearing the news. 'Now if they can just get the other guy to do it too.'

Mrs Harold Smith, who had accompanied her husband to Washington from Rochester, NY, for the acupuncture treatment, wondered 'why they bring up part of history. This happened years ago. People can change.'

Hendrik Hoestra, a professor from the University of Wageningen, The Netherlands, 'got the impression that there was too much truth in the accusations, and that the President didn't support Mr Agnew. The publicity had not been good for your country.'

Harry Nurkin, a hospital administrator from Asheville, NC, called the resignation 'unfortunate' but said it was 'better for the country than the divisiveness of fighting it through.'

Josephine Pelton of Chicago felt 'very sad, for his family that he got himself into such a mess, and for our country most of all.'

Donald P. Baker

Press suit by Agnew held moot

Spiro T. Agnew's 'no contest' plea to an income tax evasion charge automatically ended the former Vice-President's attempt to force reporters to reveal their confidential sources in articles written about the Agnew investigation.

After sentencing Agnew on Wednesday, US District Court Judge Water E. Hoffman said that the subpoenaing of nine newsmen was canceled and the anticipated major battle over the press's First Amendment rights had become moot.

Agnew's acceptance of a criminal sentence came after lawyers for the reporters had filed motions arguing that the attempt to force newsmen to reveal their sources was clearly unconstitutional and prohibited by Maryland law.

'The fact that Spiro Agnew is Vice-President gives him no special license to trample the First Amendment rights of the press and the public and to lead this court into a political jungle in an attempt to put his career in politics back together again,' Joseph A. Califano Jr., lawyer for the *Washington Post* and *Newsweek* magazine, said in his motion.

Attorneys for the *New York Times* called the court-authorized subpoenas 'a uniquely dangerous threat to the entire process of news gathering and reporting. The issue posed by these subpoenas is the very continuation of investigative reporting itself.'

In addition to subpoenaing the nine reporters, Agnew's lawyers also subpoenaed six officials: Attorney General Elliot L. Richardsons, Associate Attorney General Jonathan

Moore, Assistant Attorney General Henry Petersen, acting Assistant Attorney General Glen E. Pommerening, US Attorney for Maryland George Beall, and Barnet D. Skolnik, Beall's principal assistant prosecutor in the Agnew probe.

The subpoenas were issued in the search for evidence to support Agnew's contention that he could not get a fair trial because of press reports of the allegations against him, which he charged were deliberately 'leaked' by Justice Department officials.

The six subpoenaed Justice officials and other officials signed affidavits denying they had leaked anything.

Douglas P. Watson

'A good deal for everyone'

Assuming it was a deal that led to Spiro T. Agnew's resignation and his no-contest plea on one count of income tax evasion, it was a pretty good deal – clearly for Agnew, and quite probably for the rest of us as well.

From Agnew's point of view, the prosecutors must have had a formidable case against him. It's impossible to imagine his resigning if a single count of income tax evasion was the biggest thing they had.

Thus any arrangement whereby the bulk of the potential charges would be dropped has to be a pretty good deal for Agnew, who after all was, at the end, more concerned about saving his reputation and his freedom than about saving his job.

It may not have been a bad deal from the people's point of view either. Except for those who wanted their vengeance on Agnew, it's hard to imagine that much good would have come from putting the man in jail.

From the people's standpoint, the worst thing about Agnew was that the nature of the charges – and the nature of his reaction to them – had rendered him worthless for the only real function of his office: to succeed to the Presidency. Thus there was need to have him out of office. That he satisfied that need without the turmoil of impeachment proceedings or constitutional wrangling over his immunity from prosecution has to be a plus for the country.

To some degree, Agnew's own statement said as much. 'My decision to resign and enter a plea of *nolo contendere* rests on my firm belief that the public interest requires swift disposition of the problems which are facing me,' he said.

Nolo contendere is not an admission of guilt but rather a decision not to fight the charges – often for facesaving purposes, or to avoid vulnerability to civil action.

But in Agnew's case, he admitted to the judge that he 'did receive payments during the year 1967 which were not expended for political purposes and that, therefore, these payments were income taxable to me in that year and that I so knew'.

His plea apparently kills other potential charges against him – presumably serious charges for which there was serious evidence – and a case can be made that the deal has had the effect of thwarting justice. Well, maybe so. But I think it was better to get the thing quickly done, even if it keeps Agnew out of jail on other charges.

Two immediate problems remain: what to do about the Vice-Presidential vacancy, and what to do about the President. The links between the two are obvious.

The combination of Agnew's troubles and the tailing-off of the Senate Watergate hearings succeeded in taking nearly all the heat off President Nixon, despite the overwhelming public belief that he was implicated in the Watergate scandals, or at least in the cover-up of the scandals.

With the Agnew business out of the way, attention will return to the President, and to the question of impeachment. And that inevitably raises questions about filling the Agnew vacancy. The constitution provides that such vacancies be filled by the President, with Congressional confirmation.

The consensus here seems to be that the President would not nominate a strong Democrat lest he give the

Democrats too big an advantage in the 1976 Presidential race, and that the Democratic-controlled Congress would not approve a potential Republican candidate. Nor could the President, under attack for the poor caliber of men in his administration, afford to nominate a weak Vice-President of either party.

Probably the smartest thing Mr Nixon could do would be to nominate someone like Sen. Edward Brooke of Massachusetts. The fact that Brooke is a Republican could help him with his own party; the fact that he is an unlikely contender for the Presidency could help him with Democrats. And the fact that he is black would virtually eliminate any chance of impeachment proceedings against the President. Assassination, too for that matter.

On the other hand, while the 25th Amendment permits the Congress to pass on a Presidential nominee, it does not require the Congress to approve anyone. It may be that the best thing Congress could do would be not to accept any nominee, on the assumption that a President under threat of impeachment has no business being permitted to choose his own successor.

Failure to approve a new Vice-President would be meaningless for so long as Mr Nixon remains in office. And if he should resign or be removed, House Speaker Carl Albert might be just about as good a temporary replacement as anybody the President and the Congress are likely to agree on.

William Raspberry

Pat Nixon 'saddened'

Pat Nixon telephoned Judy Agnew yesterday to express the 'saddened feelings' of the First Family over the resignation of her husband. Vice-President Spiro T. Agnew.

Helen McCain Smith, the First Lady's Press Secretary, said Mrs Nixon told Mrs Agnew 'what a great job she had done,' and they reminisced about their five years in the public spot-light.

'Obviously it was a hard time for both of them,' Mrs Smith said.

Mrs Nixon reached Mrs Agnew at her Maryland home around 5 PM after trying to get in touch with her earlier in the afternoon.

The First Lady did not learn the news until a newscaster broke in on the National league playoff baseball game she was watching on television.

Mrs Agnew broke the news to two of her secretaries at their suburban Maryland home just before going to Baltimore.

United Press International

Yet Agnew did what needed doing

Concerning the resignation of Mr Agnew, a few observations:

Cheating on one's income tax is a deed both grubby and adventurous. The American ethic on the question is, so far as I know, unique. When the income tax was imposed in Spain for the fist time 20 years ago, tax blanks were sent to 70,000 inhabitants in Barcelona whose incomes were known to fall in the taxable levels. When deadline came, something less than 40 people sent in their completed returns.

In England (I am told) no one has ever been sent to jail for income tax evasion – instead there are discreet negotiations. In the United States, default on income tax has emerged not only as something on the order of civic profanity, but as the offense the Government gets you for when it can't find anything else. Al Capone is the traditional example.

Spiro Agnew made a stupid mistake in 1967, and he also made a mistake which, judged by American cultural ethics, was dishonorable. He made the mistake while serving as Governor of Maryland, far removed from the position he was soon to be drafted into, wherein he found himself like St. Augustine of Hippo, suddenly elevated to an episcopacy whence to anathematize those things which he had most routinely committed in his earlier years.

For Agnew the income tax chiseler I feel nothing more than the pity I feel for the pickpocket. My beef against Agnew is that he stood before the women in California as recently as a fortnight ago and swore to them that he was innocent. That is hard to explain, very hard. We have here, once again, what I have called the Profumo Factor. John Profumo did not fall in England because he presided over dreadful orgies, but because he looked the House of Commons in the eye and said that he was innocent. If there is an explanation for Spiro Agnew looking the ladies in the eye in California and saying, 'Trust in me – I am innocent,' I want to hear it. As soon as possible.

Assume that there is such an explanation... Assume that – let us conjecture – the Vice-President was benumbed, that he indulged such impulses as are stimulated by screaming loyalists and eristic lawyers who point out constructions on the basis of which one can plausibly contend that Sirhan Sirhan wasn't the man who killed Robert Kennedy, and that Spiro Agnew didn't really need to declare that particular $29,500 as income, assuming that that moral parachute is available to Spiro Agnew, certain things need to be said.

One of them is that Spiro Agnew was transformed when he became Vice-President. Suddenly he was no longer the County Executive. Agnew should be judged by history not as the tacky defalcator if 1967, but as the Vice-President of 1969–73.

And oh what a mark he made. It was said about him briefly during 1967 and 1970 that he had agreed to serve as 'Nixon's Nixon.' It is correct that he undertook to serve as the cutting edge of Nixon's Presidency, and that he got the popularity.

It is also true that he did a job that greatly needed doing during a period when the academic population was largely frozen in physical fear and intellectual paralysis. When the broad shouldered moralists of Harvard, Berkeley, Cornell and Columbia were cringing before their mindless tormentors, Agnew was reiterating the norms of civilized and democratic conduct, the norms the Lords Spiritual were supposed to be upholding, except that they were too busy: capitulating to the kids, and making fun of Spiro Agnew.

During that important period in American history Agnew distinguished himself by defending these norms, by laying blame where it belonged, by declaring in rhetoric steadfast his continuing allegiance to the ideals of liberty and order. I do not doubt that his personal influence, his personal impact, consolidated the public that came finally to stand up against the moral anarchists who, when they violated the law, whinnied out their defenses pleading the grand immunities of civil disobedience and anti-militarism.

As the dust settles on the political thoughts of Spiro Agnew one doubts that justice in the truest sense has now come to America. It is always bracing when mighty men fall. But less so when they fall for such offenses as brought Agnew down. It is ironic to meditate on the great number of those who stand erect disdaining Spiro Agnew, whose crimes against society are of a truly plausible magnitude.

William F. Buckley Jr.

By God, it hurts

In time, because all wounds heal in time, this wound will heal. But on the day after Spiro Agnew's confession and resignation, as this is written, the wound bleeds. It hurts. By God, it hurts.

I liked and admired this man; I believed in him. In print and on the hustings, I have defended Ted Agnew a thousand times these past five years. I applauded his deserved attacks upon the liberal media. I delighted in his quick wit and self deprecating humor. And because he had 'not been touched by Watergate' – what an irony is that! – I looked warmly toward his bid to the Republican nomination in 1976.

On this cold gray morning in Washington, the disillusion is total.

'I admit,' said Agnew in court, 'that I did receive payments during the year 1967 which were not expended for political purposes and that, therefore, these payments were income taxable to me in that year, and that I so knew. I further acknowledge that contracts were awarded by state agencies in 1967 and other years to those who made such payments, and that I was aware of such awards.'

In the light of that confession, it is not necessary – it merely quickens the pain – to dwell upon the sordid details etched with such cruel clarity in the Government's supporting information. It is all there: the hints, the implications, the brown manila envelopes stuffed with cash, the evidence of payments secretly made to Agnew long after he had ceased to be Governor of Maryland and had become Vice-President of the United States.

It is true, of course, as a matter of law, that these detailed charges have not been proved, and that Agnew is 'presumed innocent' of the corruption they entail. He has 'categorically denied' their truth. Such matters of law are lost in limbo now. By his own plea to the single count of tax evasion, Agnew made it impossible for the Government to prove these other charges. He himself has destroyed the presumption of innocence.

His denial chokes in the throat. Can we believe his protestation? If these other charges were in fact 'damned lies', if they were based upon perjured affidavits, if he were guiltless of any wrongdoing, what, then, was his proper course? It was to resign his office, demand trial, and fight for acquittal by a jury.

Yes, such a trial might have inflicted upon the nation, as Attorney General Richardson said, 'serious and permanent scars'. Such an ordeal, as Agnew said, would have been 'brutalizing' for his wife and children. But the nation is strong; it has survived deeper scars. Wives and children are stronger than we think; they would have endured the ordeal. Agnew's one chance for vindication, if he were indeed innocent, was to demand his day in court. On Wednesday he swapped it away.

The hurt is muffled in sorrow. For the past seven years – seven years! – Agnew has been carrying this secret weight upon his conscience. It must have lain like a stone in his belly. No matter how he moved, or joked, or tried to forget it, the lump was still there. What went through Agnew's mind, one wonders, when his friendly visitor came with the envelope in the morning, and he made a speech that night on the old values: honesty, integrity, obedience to law.

It is a lame excuse it is no excuse at all – that he had financial problems. Everybody has financial problems. As

Vice-President surely he had no need of the money we are left to assume he accepted – no need, that is, in the sense that his immigrant father had needs. Agnew could have gotten along on $72,500 a year. One is reminded of Abe Fortas; who had no need of the outside income he accepted when he served on the Supreme Court. Flawed crystal and false gold! One rues with Browning the course of lost leaders: just for a handful of silver they leave us.

No one – not the press, not Richard Nixon, not Elliot Richardson or Henry Peterson – no one compelled Agnew in 1967 to adopt 'a long-established pattern of political fund-raising in Maryland.' No one compelled him to take payments 'which were not expended for political purposes.' He himself has stained this administration, shattered his believing friends, and dealt one more blow to the crippled President who raised him from obscurity. Don't bother, Ted, to say it ain't so.

James J. Kilpatrick

Agnew's 'no contest' plea may prompt move by IRS

Spiro T. Agnew's plea of 'no contest' in the income-tax evasion case against him may mark only the beginning of difficulties for him with the Internal Revenue Service.

An IRS spokesman said yesterday that so far as the agency is aware, there is nothing in the agreement that led to Agnew's resignation as Vice-President that would prohibit IRS from attempting to collect taxes on every payment to Agnew that can be documented as having been made, but not reported on his tax returns.

The charge of tax-evasion, to which Agnew pleaded *nolo contendere*, involved $29,500. But a document released by the Justice Department detailing the evidence against the former Vice-President alleges payments from contractors and others totaling $87,500.

The precise figure is not clear, because some of the allegations of illegal payments are stated in terms of percentages of the values of construction contracts awarded, and the figures for the contracts themselves are not given.

The IRS spokesman said, however, that it was common in tax-evasion cases for a charge of criminal tax-evasion to be made involving a relatively small figure and for a civil action to come later involving a much larger figure. There is no statue of limitations for civil tax fraud.

Generally, the official explained, the reason is that much higher standards of proof must be met in criminal cases.

Agnew's no-contest plea could, however, help him in fighting any future civil case, one tax expert said.

In pleading no contest, a defendant prevents the Government from relying on the criminal prosecutors' evidence and forces it to the burdensome and lengthy job of building a separate civil case.

There was no indication last night whether the Government will open a civil tax case.

Persons familiar with the enforcement of the tax laws also noted that Agnew was not necessarily being given exceptional treatment in being merely fined $10,000 and not jailed. The $10,000 is the maximum fine, per count of tax violation, provided by law, but jail terms of up to five years are also specified.

Fewer than half of all the persons convicted of criminal tax violations in the fiscal year that ended last June 30 were jailed IRS figures show.

Eileen Shanahan

Agnew seen retaining civil rights but the IRS and Maryland are expected to file tax actions

US Attorney General Elliot L. Richardson said yesterday he thinks it is unlikely that Spiro T. Agnew will lose any of his civil rights – which include the rights to vote and hold office – because he pleaded 'no contest' rather than guilty to a Federal tax evasion charge.

But the question of whether the former Vice-President forfeited any of his civil rights by entering the plea remains unresolved and may ultimately be answered by officials in Baltimore County, where Agnew got his start in politics.

Loss of certain rights is just one of the prospects facing Agnew as a private citizen who Wednesday surrendered the second highest office in the nation, was fined $10,000 and placed on unsupervised probation for three years.

He is expected to face civil actions by both the Internal Revenue Service and the State of Maryland to recover thousands in allegedly unpaid income taxes. 'If taxes are owed we go after them,' said an IRS spokesman of the agency's general policy.

Agnew also faces a probable move in Maryland to disbar him as a lawyer, according to bar association leaders.

He could be subject to state criminal prosecution there but Richardson and Maryland attorney General Francis B. Burch yesterday recommended against state prosecution and it is not likely.

Richardson flatly ruled out further Federal prosecution of Agnew.

For the time being Agnew continues to be protected by Secret Service agents. Employees in the Vice-President's office continued at work yesterday, wondering how long their jobs will last.

Agnew will not receive a Federal pension not because of his courtroom plea, but because he did not work as a Federal employee for the required five year minimum period. He will receive refunds on any pension payments he made as Vice-President, a Civil service Commission spokesman said.

Richardson told a press conference at the Justice Department yesterday that because Agnew pleaded *nolo contendere*, which means no contest, rather than guilty to the tax evasion charge, he will not lose the rights normally denied convicted felons.

On the issue of civil rights, Deputy Maryland Attorney General Henry Lord said last night that 'there's a serious question as to whether there's been a conviction at all for purposes of the Maryland Constitution.'

He said any questions regarding possible forfeiture of these rights in Maryland will have to be decided on a piecemeal basis, by the governmental bodies that adjudicate such rights.

Questions about Agnew's voting rights Lord said, fall 'completely within the purview of the board of election supervisors of Baltimore County.'

Persons convicted of felonies are normally deprived of the right to vote. But Lord said that there is a question in Agnew's case 'whether the crime involved is an infamous crime under the Maryland constitution.' If it is determined to be such a crime, Agnew would be deprived of his voting rights.

Walter Ballesteros, an attorney for the Baltimore County Board of Election supervisors, said: 'In my opinion, I don't think a ('no contests') plea is the same as a guilty plea, but that's just an off hand observation.'

'I think there would have to be a meeting (of the three-member board to issue a ruling on Agnew's rights). We've never had a case like this,' Ballesteros said last night.

Richardson further said that Maryland's Constitution does not bar Agnew from holding office there because of his plea.

When asked whether Agnew would be free to travel abroad, Richardson said, 'Since the judge made clear that the probation would be unsupervised... I suppose that Mr Agnew would be free to live where he chooses.

Asked whether Agnew could be prosecuted in Maryland on state charges involving similar allegations to those made by the Justice Department, Richardson said, 'There is nothing in the agreement (with Agnew) that would prevent action by state prosecutors.'

But, Richardson continued, 'My own hope would be that it would be considered by state prosecutors as it is by the Federal prosecution: that the public interest is now best served by considering the matter to have been dealt with on a basis of fairness and justice and the public interest.'

Maryland Attorney General Burch seconded Richardson's statements, saying it would be unwise 'to drag this thing (the Agnew allegations) over the coals again and again.' Burch pointed out though that any decision on state prosecution will by law be made by local state's attorneys and not his office.

Baltimore County State's Attorney Samuel A. Green Jr., himself presently under indictment on bribery charged said, 'The Vice-President has suffered enough' and that he was more interested in pursuing Agnew's associates.

In regard to Agnew's tax problems, IRS officials declined to say specifically whether civil action will be taken against the former Vice-President to recover taxes he conceded in court he did not pay. They noted IRS's rules on confidentiality.

Bar leaders, while declining to prejudice Agnew's case, predicted that disciplinary action would be instituted against Agnew even though… as one lawyer put it 'it will be a very distasteful duty.'

Douglas Watson,
B.D. Colen

'He resigned because he had no choice.'

Vice-President Spiro Agnew's sudden, secret approach to the Justice Department last Friday to renew his plea bargaining not only surprised Federal prosecutors but also followed two weeks during which they had no new communications at all with Agnew.

It was during those two weeks, following his defiant speech in Los Angeles, that Agnew sought to generate national sympathy by portraying himself as a victim of a Justice Department plot.

Thus, Agnew's new approach on Oct. 5 to Justice Department prosecutors – an approach made without the knowledge of some of his closest advisers – was interpreted by high administration officials as a signal that the Vice-President's national campaign had failed totally. In fact, he did not receive terms substantially better than he could have received some three weeks earlier.

The overriding view is that Agnew resigned because he had no choice and simply could not carry through with the battle to remain in office in the face of Federal prosecution. That greatly reduces prospects of the Agnew affair seriously damaging President Nixon in the hearts of Republican right-wingers mourning their departed leader.

When Attorney General Elliot Richardson and his lieutenants several weeks ago discussed strategy on how to handle the charges against Agnew, the possibility of an Agnew counterattack against them was mentioned. It was the Vice-President's style, all agreed to try to recover by attacking his accusers.

The possibility of such a counter attack was enhanced when the first round of plea bargaining between Agnew's lawyers and the Justice Department broke down. One basic disagreement: The prosecutors insisted upon full disclosure of the evidence against the Vice-President.

Ambivalent from the start about whether to fight the charges or quit, Agnew began to accept advice from those lieutenants who wanted him to fight. The result was his Sept. 29 speech in Los Angeles pledging that he would not resign even if indicted and assaulting the Justice Department (particularly Assistant Attorney General Henry Petersen) as the source of his woes. Next came his legal efforts to force newsmen to reveal the sources of leaks about the case.

This campaign is now being viewed by some politicians as a blatant attempt to force better terms out of the Justice Department. 'Utter nonsense,' retorts one high Justice Department official. Rather, knowledgeable friends and foes generally agree that Agnew was trying to enlist public opinion on his side in hopes of generating pressure against the Government.

He was only partially successful. Some Republican stalwarts, resentful that the President undermined his Vice-President, rushed to Agnew's defense. Furthermore, Agnew made his point about leaks to news media undermining his case and eroding his civil liberties, but he was clearly unable to convince the country that there was a conscious conspiracy, centered in the Justice Department, to drive him out of office.

Indeed, polling data and politicians' insights indicate that the public would not tolerate Agnew staying in office while indicted. With Agnew having failed to convince the public he was a victim, the voters were unwilling to grant his special immunity.

After what one White House aide described as 'an ordeal of unbelievable magnitude,' Agnew advised his lawyers to resume plea bargaining (the approach that came Oct. 5). Agnew kept that fact from all but his closest associates. Only Arthur Sohmer, his longtime assistant from Maryland days, and possibly Brig. Gen. John M. Dunn, his highly trusted military aide, knew about it.

In the renewed plea bargaining, Agnew's lawyers this time accepted the Justice Department demands for a full disclosure on the case against him (resulting in the 40-page paper released Wednesday). Agnew's lawyers asked for an assurance of leniency. The Justice Department could give no such assurance but promised it would recommend leniency to the judge. The recommendation was made and accepted.

The result was that Agnew saved the nation from another protracted political crisis and perhaps saved himself from a prison sentence – but at the cost of his name and his disillusioned political following. With the failure of his campaign to show himself as the Justice Department's persecuted victim, there was no other outcome.

Rowland Evans,
Robert Novak

District takes news with cynicism, gloom

After months and months of reading and hearing about Watergate and stories of corruption, the resignation yesterday of Vice-President Spiro T. Agnew came to Washingtonians only as something to be taken in stride – another example of the nature of politics.

'I think it's the state of affairs throughout the whole country,' Gerry McGurry, 39, a bartender at the Marquee Lounge in the Shoreham Hotel, said. 'It's unfortunate,' he added.

Speaking with the kind of logic that seems second nature to bartenders and cab drivers, McCurry, a Democrat, said, 'If the Watergate thing wasn't around, I think it (charges against Agnew) would have been hushed.'

'A lot worse things have been thrown under the bed,' McCurry said, speaking about charges of income tax evasion lodged against Agnew.

'I don't fault him for trying to get away with it 'cause everybody else does it,' doorman Joe Heurick said about the charges.

However, 'I feel that if he got caught, he ought to resign,' Heurick said at the Shoreham. 'His biggest sin was getting caught.'

John G. Barker, President of Marshall University, and John S. Callebs, a political scientist and Vice-President of Bethany College, here for an educational conference as representative of the West Virginia College, were fearful of the possible effects Agnew's resignation will have on the political system.

'It undermines the public confidence,' Barker said. 'I think that's the greatest danger to the country,' he added.

Callebs was concerned that a fight over a successor to Agnew could 'split the nation'. Agnew said he hoped his resignation would prevent such a situation.

'I'm not shocked or surprised,' by the Agnew resignation, one young woman said in the lounge of the Pitts Motor Hotel in Northwest.

Speaking above a loud rhythm and blues record being played by a disc jockey, James Hodnott, 24, suggested that President Nixon nominate a black for the Vice-Presidency to gain black support of the Republican national ticket in 1976.

Although most of the 20 persons interviewed expressed a pessimistic attitude toward politics in general, several said they felt betrayed by Agnew's resignation.

'I thought he was the finest one we had in politics,' Eddie Frank 25, night waiter in a Wisconsin Avenue Toddle House, said.

Frank said he wasn't surprised that corruption exists in national politics, even in the White House, but 'I can't really believe the way that they got him.'

Some people saw a political plot to eliminate the Vice-President as a potential Presidential candidate in 1976.

Robert Lane, 32, a limousine driver, said the investigation of Agnew was the first step toward impeachment of Nixon.

'I think they were trying to get Agnew out of the way so they can get Nixon,' he said. 'They didn't want Agnew as President.'

Helen King, a waitress at the Toddle House, said: 'I'm ashamed of the whole Nixon administration.'

John Robinson, a 35-year old tow truck driver, said: 'Tricky Dick should have gone with him (Agnew),' expressing a feeling that Nixon was involved in political misbehavior.

Robinson, who was not alone in believing that Agnew was sacrificed for political expediency, said, 'I think he's out of there 'cause Nixon put him out of there.'

John C. White

Three months short Resignation cost pension

Spiro Agnew failed by three months to become eligible for a civil service annuity that would have been worth about $15,000 a year to him once he reached 62.

Had the 54-year-old Agnew remained in office as Vice-President until Jan 20, he would have competed the minimum 5 years of service eligibility required for civil service pensions.

Agnew's no contest plea to the 1967 income tax evasion charge had nothing to do with his failure to qualify for an annuity.

Under the law conviction of a criminal offense does not bar a government official or employee from an annuity unless it involved treason, espionage or other grave offenses involving national security.

Had Agnew completed five years of Federal service, he could have added his approximately five years of military service, for a total of 10 years for annuity computation purposes. But military service cannot be counted for a civil service pension unless an official or employee first acquires the five years of civilian Government service.

However, Agnew can get a refund of the civil service retirement contributions he made while Vice-President. This will amount to about $22,000.

Joseph Young

All due reverent speed

The Agnew Affair, following on the Eagleton Affair, suggests again that the normal procedures for selecting Vice-Presidential candidates in American have been almost criminally negligent, so maybe they should be examined before President Nixon picks a successor for Spiro Agnew.

The system – if that's the word for it – has produced some good accidental Presidents, notably Theodore Roosevelt, Harry Truman, Lyndon Johnson, and maybe Chester A. Arthur, who succeeded the murdered James A. Garfield, but it has also produced quite a few dubs, who were chosen too fast and usually for the wrong reasons.

Eagleton was picked by George McGovern at the last minute over the telephone in 1972, and everybody knows what happened there. But even now, we don't know much about how Agnew was selected by Nixon in 1968, or who, if anybody, checked his record before he was sprung on a surprised Republican convention.

The situation now, of course, is different. The President cannot impose his new man on the House and Senate, as he imposed Agnew on an obedient party in 1968 and 1972, but he still seems to be in a hell of a hurry to find a successor, before people have had time to think about what kind of successor the country needs.

During the last World War in London, there was a modest sign along the aisles in Westminster Cathedral. 'In the event of an air raid,' it said 'parishioners will descend to the crypts with all due reverent speed.' That is not a bad guide to the present. Take it seriously, but take it easy.

Nixon is seeking advice from everyone around here about the person to be chosen as Vice-President, as he did in 1968. He paid no attention to the advice he was given. He has asked for names in sealed envelopes by this weekend, which is not a bad idea, so what's the hurry?

Washington is both sad and angry about Agnew. His friends feel he has let them down, and even his enemies feel both that he got off too easy, but that he was punished more severely than others guilty of more serious offenses, if not crimes. Nobody has yet had time to sort out the past, let alone to be clear about the future.

Maybe then, this is a time for little judicious leaving alone. There is no emergency. The President may be preoccupied with Agnew's problems and his own problems, but the Government is carrying on, and carrying on with a better Cabinet than it has had for years.

Ironically, it is being carried on in large part by a few Harvard types, inky jobs, who used to be the enemies of Nixon, Agnew, and Middle America – Kissinger at State, Schlesinger at Defense, Richardson at Justice, Cox as special prosecutor, Dunlop on the economy. It would be funny if it weren't so serious, but anyway, the Republic will probably survive even if it doesn't have a new Vice-President next week, or even next month.

This time, there is a chance to ask the right questions, and check out the answers. Eagleton and Agnew were nominated for the Vice-Presidency, not because they were Presidential figures, or even because they had much to contribute to the ticket, but because they were attractive nonentities, who were probably acceptable to the party or labor powers because they were unknown. Nobody concentrated on the question of character.

This casual cynicism has cost both parties much more than they imagined, and it will be interesting to see now whether the President has learned the lesson of the Agnew and Eagleton disasters. Essentially, they were failures of character, and not of politics.

The President is being urged on the one hand to nominate the best potential chief executive he can find, even if this tilts the 1976 Presidential nomination toward the man of his choice, and on the other hand, to pick, a competent caretaker, who will not run in 1976 and will be quickly confirmed and avoid more controversy, which nobody needs or wants.

There is a good argument on both sides of this question and Washington is obviously divided about the answer. So it needs time to sort things out. After Johnson and Nixon, after the tragedies of Eagleton and Agnew, maybe the country needs nothing more than a simple man of character, who will be plain and honest. But Washington is not thinking about this. It is not only confused for the moment about the answer, but about the question. It needs time to remember the tragedies of Eagleton and Agnew, and consider, for a chance, the future of the Republic.

James Reston

Mr Agnew's resignation

When a proud, aggressive and supremely confident politician, such as Spiro Agnew, falls from his estate, one necessarily feels compassion for the man – and that is true irrespective of what may have caused his fall. On the occasion of Mr Agnew's resignation from the Vice-Presidency as a result of his alleged involvement in criminal activities, one must also feel a particular measure of sympathy for the constituency he had come to represent, those men and women who earnestly believed him to be a voice of reason, tradition and no-nonsense moral rigor in the hullabaloo of contemporary American life. And, in a different sense, one feels for the country too, the much put upon electorate that must experience this particular convulsion at the end of a series of so many disillusionments and disappointments and outright tragedies over the past decade.

From all three points of view, however – that of Mr Agnew, that of his special political following and that of the country as a whole – it seems to us that Mr Agnew has taken the wisest and best course available to him in pleading *nolo contendere* to a single tax evasion count and stepping out of office in exchange for dropping of the other counts against him. Attorney General Richardson put it right: 'By his resignation he has spared the nation the prolonged agony that would have attended upon his trial.' In this connection we would add that the Justice Department was equally well-advised in negotiating the agreement which

Mr Agnew accepted. The public interest could hardly have been served by a remorseless pursuit of conviction and penalty at the expense of a relatively speedy resolution of questions concerning the vitality of the second highest office in the land. Mr Agnew was Vice-President. He stood to inherit the Presidency at any moment in the event that Richard Nixon could no longer fulfill its functions. It would have been intolerable for that office to have been held by a man under criminal indictment and in process of waging a prolonged legal battle against Federal prosecutors in the courts.

From the outset – which is to say, from the time the investigation of his conduct was made public – Mr Agnew, as a man holding a very great public trust, had but two choices. One was effectively and definitively to deny and disprove the charges against him. For all his expostulations and 'damned lies' and the rest, he never chose to take this course – either in public statements he might have issued or in evidence he might have elected to present in an actual trial. His other choice was to do what he has now done, namely, to concede at least some of the evidence against him and to remove himself from office. If he did not actually have a wholly persuasive airtight defense, he could only have lost more than he could possibly have gained by stringing the affair out in a battle of court maneuvers.

These are important facts to understand, for the aftermath of the Agnew resignation may be a particularly volatile time in our political life, and it is essential that we grasp what it is that has happened to Mr Agnew. He has not been 'hounded' out of office or misused by the Justice Department or denied the fair trial that is every citizen's right or made a scapegoat for Watergate in some convoluted internal White House maneuver. On this last score, especially, it is important to note that Mr Agnew almost accidentally fetched up in the net of prosecutors in

Maryland who had undertaken initially to investigate the behavior of certain contractors, engineers and Maryland office holders in both parties. And whatever high level administration maneuvering went on once Mr Agnew's predicament came to public attention, his resignation from office – though perhaps a necessity and perhaps a temporary diversion from other Washington follies – can hardly be regarded as a long-term political plus for Mr Nixon.

In addition to the suspicions that he was hounded unfairly from office, there seems to be a fairly widespread feeling around that Mr Agnew was inequitably dealt with because 'everyone' in politics does what he was accused of doing. The former Vice-President himself, in another political time, was a most voluble critic of this and related lines of thought, which he denounced under the heading of 'permissiveness'. Surely, it would be a final cruel and demeaning twist of fate for his friends and supporters now to take up this irrelevant argument. In the first place 'everyone' doesn't do it. In the second place, everyone isn't Vice-President.

The most dangerous aspect of the solution negotiated by the Justice Department and Mr Agnew is the fact that necessarily so many particular questions have been left judicially unanswered. The danger is that the public will now be treated to new wars over the implications of those unanswered questions, with Mr Agnew claiming on the one side that the evidence put forward by the Justice Department was not just untested in court but demonstrably malicious and false, and with others receiving these charges as demonstrable proved truth. The charges themselves are pretty fierce and pretty disheartening, but one should remember two things about them. One is that they were not subjected to the test of a courtroom trial. The other is that they were not tested in a courtroom because Mr Agnew chose that they not be.

Americans don't much care for ambiguity. And politicians and public officials don't much care for having it thought on any occasion that they were wrong or irresponsible – or worse. So it will not be surprising if a painful dispute ensues over the 'real meaning' of the Justice Department's recitation of its evidence and the subsequent resignation of Mr Agnew. But it will be no less unfortunate for that. The unanswered questions are in fact a condition of the solution that has been reached, and that solution has salvaged what dignity and integrity there was to be salvaged for the processes of government in an unprecedented ugly situation. The benefits to the public that accrue from that solution are fragile and vulnerable to political recklessness. We think it is in everyone's interest, including Mr Agnew's, that they be preserved.

Editorial Comment
The *Washington Post*

Choosing the new Vice-President

President Nixon has begun the process of selecting a new Vice-President in a sensible, reassuring way by soliciting recommendations from his fellow Republicans. Mr Nixon's penchant for deliberating over large decisions has seldom been more appropriate, for the circumstances in which the vacancy must be filled could hardly be more momentous or more mischief-prone. A lame-duck President, with his administration under several clouds, must nominate a new Vice-President to be confirmed by a Congress run by the opposition party. It is a situation which will test the maturity and statesmanship of everyone involved – the President, the Congress and the eventual nominee.

Some have suggested that Mr Nixon should, in one sense, minimize the political consequences of his choice by nominating a caretaker Vice-President, someone who is generally acceptable or unobjectionable, and who either has no Presidential ambitions or is willing to renounce those ambitions to serve for little more than two years in the second seat. This, in our view is a frivolous and unwise approach. The principal qualification for a new Vice-President is fitness to assume the Presidency if need be. This means that the nominee should possess, to the greatest possible extent, that blend of ability, experience, energy and public confidence which suits an individual to take command. The human fact is that anyone who even approaches such a capacity will be, pretty much by definition, one who also possesses the ambition, drive and self-esteem which propel people to become Presidential aspirants.

Thus to require a Shermanesque renunciation of ambition as the price of confirmation would so narrow the field that the nation would likely be deprived of the best candidates. It would also insure that the new Vice-President, if called on to assume the Presidency before 1977, would be a lame duck from the start. Indeed, such a person might be able to do little more than keep the Government running in the most routine, minimal way – at precisely the time when new vitality and forcefulness would be most urgently required.

A notion which raises even more objections is that which suggests the nomination not be made, or if made should be dealt with by the Congress, until the issue of the tapes have been resolved or the uncertainties about the future of the Nixon administration have been removed by some other climactic event. But even the remote possibility of impeachment proceedings against Mr Nixon at some future date increases the importance of naming a new Vice-President now, so that at least that one troublesome question will have been resolved. In the worst of cases, prolonging the vacancy could place the Speaker of the House in the position of arranging, through his influence on impeachment proceedings, his own elevation to the Presidency. Yet the whole thrust and purpose of the 25th Amendment was to preclude such Byzantine occurrence.

In sum, the nomination should be made by Mr. Nixon and considered by the Congress with dispatch, though not with haste. Toward that end, the congressional leadership should spell out without delay the exact procedures to be employed. In the House, there seems to be general agreement that the nomination will go to the Committee on the Judiciary. In the Senate, however, there is a great potential for confusion in the competing claims of the Rules and Judiciary Committees. While the Rules Committee has exercised jurisdiction over the housekeeping aspects of presidential succession in the past, the Judiciary Committee has a valid claim by virtue of its larger membership and considerable experience in weighing nominations to the Supreme Court. The clash might best be resolved by creating a special committee whose membership would be broadly representative of the senate at large. By settling such procedural issues now, the Congress can be prepared to start its deliberations in an orderly and serious way as soon as President Nixon reaches his decision and submits the most important nomination he may ever make.

Editorial Staff Writer
The *Washington Post*

Paying attention to Watergate

Because the public memory can be so distressingly short, a few reminders may be in order:

1. The fact that Spiro Agnew has resigned does not mean that the country is out of the woods of scandal.
2. The fact that the recent revelations of the Senate Watergate committee are less startling than some of the earlier ones does not mean that the case against the Administration is weaker than it used to be.
3. The fact that the public mind has latched on to the White House tapes as the crucial evidence as to presidential culpability does not mean that there is no case against the President without the tapes.

It's awfully hard to give adequate attention to more than one scandal at a time, and for so long as Agnew's troubles were on the front pages, because dramatic things were happening, it was easy to forget about Watergate.

But just because the Agnew case was so dramatic, it will be tempting now that it is over to breathe a big sigh of relief, choose a new Vice President and consider the Union saved. It is a temptation that ought to be resisted. The nation's real interest lies in turning full attention to the main attraction – Nixon and Watergate – now that they have closed the 'side show,' as Herblock put it last week.

But even apart from the intervention of the Agnew scandal, there is something disturbing about the way the

Watergate investigation – the Senate's public investigation, at least – is going. Because it started off on television, it had a lot of us reacting as to a TV show: we expected each new revelation to lead us inexorably toward the denouement.

We knew enough about drama to know that there would be slow periods, to emphasize the fast ones – a matter of pace. But in general, we let ourselves expect a build-up of suspense, an occasional red herring, another major piece of the puzzle and then – Aha!

That's TV. Life doesn't always unfold that way. In the case of Nixon and Watergate, the big pieces of the puzzle fell in fairly early and we were left with the solution somewhere in Act I. We're now in Act II, and we're confused.

We're confused because in TV drama, we learn to reject any answer that appears too early in the play. We're accustomed to having the solution at the end. And since the Watergate is still unfolding, we imaging that the denouement is yet to come.

It may be necessary to the committee's work to tie the last of the loose ends together: the dirty tricks, both the illegal ones and those that were the only immoral. But then it will be necessary for Sam Ervin and Co. to make their summation, to tell us what we've learned (and perhaps forgotten) during the months of hearings.

Let them remind us that we're supposed to believe that President Nixon knew nothing of the burglaries committed, promises made, lies told and funds illegally collected in his name and on his behalf.

Let them remind us that we're expected to believe that John Mitchell, who had served the President as his chief legal officer, campaign chief, friend and confidant, knew, by his own account, that some campaign officials were planning something like the Watergate break-in; that the break-in occurred; that Mitchell subsequently resigned as campaign director, and that Mitchell never told the President – and the President never asked – what he knew about what was going on.

Let them remind us of the mind-set of the men Richard Nixon chose to be his top advisors, of their cavalier attitude toward such things as subverting government agencies, burglarizing doctor's offices, circulating enemy lists and making illegal wire taps in the name of 'national security.'

Let them remind us that the only conceivable way the President could have remained ignorant of all these things was by choosing to remain ignorant, and remind us, too, that John Dean, who has reason to know, says he wasn't so ignorant after all.

Let them remind us that it is not only inconceivable that the President was unaware of the cover-up but that, by his own account, he ordered strict limitations on the official investigation into his own 'plumbers' role in the affair. He did so, he said, to avoid revealing the 'national security' work the plumbers were involved in. But that statement is the only evidence that they were involved in any national security work whatever.

And finally, let the Ervin committee or somebody remind us that all these things were established long before we even knew of the existence of the tapes. The tapes may be helpful in the case against Richard Nixon, but we shouldn't kid ourselves that they are vital.

William Raspberry

Ford got 90-minute notice 'The President is Calling'

President Nixon played it close to his vest all day and then staged a television spectacular to announce his nomination of Gerald R. Ford to be vice president.

Even Ford did not know he was the nominee until some 90 minutes before the President told the nation and an applauding audience in the White House East Room.

Other congressional leaders were informed of Ford's selection just before they walked into the East Room with him amid applause and fanfare from the Marine Orchestra.

Gen. Alexander M. Haig Jr., the White House chief of staff, was the only person who admitted that he was told of Ford's selection by the President before Ford himself knew.

It was Haig who informed Ford.

Haig told reporters that he was with the President in his Executive Office building office at 7:30 last night when the President placed a call to Ford's home.

Ford said the White House operator told him 'The President is calling,' and then Nixon came on the line and said 'I think Al Haig has some news for you.'

Then, at the President's direction, Haig suggested to Ford that his wife might want to hear what he was going to say. Betty Ford was talking at the time on another line to their oldest son, Michael, 23, a student at Gordon Conwell Divinity School in Boston.

Ford got her on the line with the White House and Haig said 'I am very pleased to notify you and your wife that the

President will nominate you to be the next vice president of the United states.'

As Haig recalled it, Ford said he was very honored and Mrs. Ford said 'This is wonderful.'

The President had told Ford yesterday morning, when he called him in for a discussion of congressional procedures in handling such a nomination, that he was one of those under consideration. But Ford said he did not know he was the man selected until the 7:30 PM telephone call. 'I guess in retrospect if I had been smarter I would have anticipated it.'

As it was, he said he had just finished his evening swim and his 16 year old daughter, Susan, was cooking steaks for dinner when he got the call.

As Ford, House Speaker Carl Albert, House Democratic leader Thomas P. O'Neill Jr. And Senate Republican leader Hugh Scott lined up in the White House Green Room to walk into the East Room just before 9 PM. Haig told the group that the President was going to name Ford. Others said Ford acted surprised at the time.

The television show started with a fanfare from the Marine orchestra in the reception area leading into the East Room and an announcement that cabinet members were entering. Then the congressional leaders were announced and walked down another aisle. Then came the announcement of the President and Mrs. Nixon and 'Hail to the Chief.'

The room was crowded with members of the Senate and the house, in addition to the cabinet, the White House Senior staff, and a few wives. Two Republican governors were there – Linwood Holton of Virginia and Daniel J. Evans of Washington.

Garnet D. Horner

The choice of Mr. Ford

For a man who spends so much time instructing the American public about what is and what is not 'appropriate' – Mr. Nixon's favorite word – the President has demonstrated an abysmal failure to comprehend the true nature of the occasion to which he addressed himself Friday night. You would not have known from the festive glitter and spirit of 'fun' in the East Room that the President was announcing his choice for the 40th Vice President of the United States because the man he had twice chosen to be the 39th Vice President had two days earlier left the office in disgrace and been convicted of a felony. You would not have known that this was only the latest evidence of corruption in high places and of a cynical breach of public trust to which a benumbed electorate had been treated over many months. Again, you would not have known that the somber duty of the President, confronted with a crisis of confidence in government was to offer a candidate for consideration of both houses of congress – not to preside over a ceremony combining the more synthetic elements of apolitical convention with the trappings of a state occasion at least worthy of the ruling house of Ruritania. And finally, you would not have guessed from the quick and automatic effusions of legislators in both parties that the 25th Amendment to the Constitution, which authorizes the President to fill vice-presidential vacancies, also imposes upon congress a heavy responsibility for subjecting his choice to serious, sustained scrutiny by way of introducing some measure of public participation in a decision of such enormous potential consequence.

We are not suggesting that the President needed to be lugubrious – only serious. And we are not suggesting that the members of Congress should have been obstructive – only restrained. We are suggesting only that there was an opportunity to embark upon precisely the 'new beginning' that the President proclaimed. But for such a 'new beginning' to have meant anything, it would have had to mean a marked departure from the cynicism, contrivance, hypocrisy and politics-as-usual which have got us into so much trouble in the recent past and which were so dishearteningly in evidence in Friday night's ceremony in the so-called selection process, and in the legislators' reflective response. The President and his congressional claque (on both sides of both aisles) would have us believe that Mr. Nixon seriously solicited suggestions from a broad cross-section of his party; that he took a crammed suggestion box off to camp David; that he deliberated long and hard overnight to determine who was the one man in the nation best fit to assume the office of the presidency on a moment's notice; and that all this led ineluctably to the name of – Gerald Ford.

Will no one be straightforward about what has been done? It is true that traditionally our Vice Presidents are selected in a reckless and haphazard manner, under heavy pressure of time and perceived political needs not necessarily related to fitness for the job. And it is equally true that by this tradition, Mr. Ford is no less qualified than many who have been chosen. But that is just the point. Both the process established by constitutional amendment for replacement of a Vice President in mid-term and the dismal circumstances that culminated in Mr. Agnew's resignation conferred upon the President an opportunity –

indeed an obligation – to break free of that sorry tradition and to choose a man for no other reason than his genuine fitness and distinction. And if one *is* to be straightforward, it must be said that Gerald Ford is not such a man. For over 25 years he has pursued a congressional career of modest ambition and modest achievement. At no point has he shown a keen or impressive grasp of the complexities of hard questions. Pedestrian, partisan, dogged he has been the very model of a second-level party man. It is no accident that over his quarter century of unremarkable service in the House, he has never been put forward seriously as a candidate for the presidency – or laid serious claim to the office on his own behalf.

The interesting thing about this characterization of Mr. Ford is that it is shared privately by many of those legislators who publicly hailed his nomination in the most extravagant terms the other night. Partly this is because the old congressional back-scratching machine works round the clock, and partly it is because the Democrats – and some Republican aspirants to higher office – found enormous comfort in the nomination of a man who, by contrast with some other prospects, represents so minimal a threat to their chances in 1976.

There is nothing laudable or uplifting about this congressional response. What makes it the more dispiriting is the near certainty that it was precisely in anticipation of such a self-serving, conventional and narrowly political response that the President made his choice. So cynicism is compounded. We are back where we began.

The *Washington Post*

Loyalty is rewarded

On too many occasions these past five years, this observer of the Washington scene has felt compelled to ask: 'Where does President Nixon find them?'

Spiro T. Agnew, G. Harold Carswell, John Ehrlichman, John Mitchell. G. Gordon Liddy.

If anything has distinguished this administration more than the breadth and magnitude of crime and corruption that has permeated it, it has to be Nixon's dogged knack for clinging to people whose ideological quirks are his own.

In nominating rep. Gerald R. Ford to be the next vice president, Nixon rose above the Carswell mediocrity. In Ford he chose a man who, by the known record, bears no taint of the crookedness and corruption that has engulfed so many of Nixon's other men.

Ford surely will win speedy confirmation – perhaps faster than I can get this column into print.

But we must not let the 'loyalty of the club' that will produce so many ayes in congress blind us to the fact that Ford's foremost claim to the Nixon wand was his steadfast support of Nixon proposals, Nixon vetoes, Nixon evasions.

The naming of Ford is dismaying evidence that Richard Nixon still thinks the measure of a man's greatness is his loyalty to Richard Nixon.

According to records compiled by Congressional Quarterly, of all the votes in congress on which Nixon won or lost from Jan. 3 to Aug. 3, in both 1972 and 1973, only one man in the entire congress was more blindly loyal to the President than Gerry Ford.

Ford voted for Nixon's position eighty-three percent of the time. Compare that with a mere sixty-eight percent 'loyalty' on the part of Roman Hruska, the Nebraska senator who enshrined himself in the history books by backing the Carswell nomination to the Supreme court with the argument that the country needs a little mediocrity.

Of the 535 people in congress, only Barber B. Conable Jr., of Alexander NY, beat Ford out (Conable was eighty-four percent loyal) for the sycophant-of-the-year award.

Nixon's failure to nominate Conable as the new veep must surely arise from the fact that the President like most Americans, never heard of Conable.

But they've heard of Ford... leading a move to impeach. Supreme court Justice William Douglas... out-Nixoning Nixon with rhetoric against school busing after the President chose to make 'forced busing' a phony but emotional campaign issue... fighting to sustain a Nixon veto of a bill that would have made the director of the Office of Management and Budget subject to senate confirmation, although Ford surely knows that this is one of the six or so most powerful jobs in the entire executive branch. Workers and maids and the laboring poor will remember Ford fighting to sustain the Nixon veto of the minimum wage bill, or the emergency Medical Services bill.

Ford's toadying role as House minority leader will arouse passionate opposition around the country, but not enough to make his fellow club members vote against him.

Still, let us not forget that the naming of a new vice president is about as important to the nation as naming a new waterboy for the Washington Redskins – unless some calamity befalls the President.

Naming Ford has extra meaning because this President faces more than the usual actuarial threats to his tenure. The court of Appeals has ordered Nixon to yield the Watergate tapes to the federal court. The odds are now overwhelming that even after Supreme court consideration the President will have to make a choice of handing over tapes that could implicate him in several felonies, or of defying an order of the highest tribunal.

Either route would lead to impeachment of Nixon or his decision to resign.

Either outcome would make Ford the president of these United States.

Impeachment now seems more than remotely possible. But resignation? Nixon has insisted that he will not resign. But then, so did the man whose job Ford is taking.

Carl T. Rowan

Explaining away Agnew's tragedy

Spiro Agnew sat in the WRC studios ready to give his last speech, the one that nobody wanted to hear. At best, it would be a blustering assertion of innocence that few would credit; at worst, a pitiful admission of guilt that few could stomach.

At 7:30 an Anacin commercial came on; then a VO 5 hair-dressing ad; finally, a sepulchral voice announced that *Hollywood Squares* would not be seen in order to bring us 'Mr. Spiro T. Agnew.' It was a typical enough prelude to televised drama: the invitation to certain headache relief, the promise of ever-better grooming, the glum news that still another fatuous TV sitcom had been knocked off the air for one more reminder of the hollowness at the center of the American political system.

Agnew came on as gray as black and white TV could make a man look. He was, in essence, faced with a question of net worth. The Justice Department evidence against him was devastating, had, on its face, that ring of verisimilitude that all too few government documents possess. It persuasively narrated a persistent pattern of Agnew-inspired kickback arrangements that traced, over a period of a decade, nearly $90,000 into the ex-vice president's personal coffers.

Outside the Baltimore courthouse last Wednesday, Agnew had denied the summary government charges against him.

Last night he merely repeated those lame professions of innocence – professions that were remarkable for the strength and precision of verbs and adverbs and the evasive vagueness of subjects and predicates. 'I flatly and categorically deny...' trickled off into the 'accusations published and broadcast as fact.' That was another way of saying that the media allegations aired against him were substantially correct, if perhaps not absolutely exact. It was, in the end, not the narrow truthfulness of the Justice department case against him that erred, but the narrow truthfulness of the charges leaded into the media. The petty crook was reduced to petty quibbling about semantics.

This woefully thin counterattack – focusing on the niceties rather than the substance of the criminal charges assembled against him – dominated the first half of Agnew's speech. It was followed by a lengthy peroration on the virtues of the Nixon administration. 'I can only see good ahead. We are within the chance of lasting peace.' The 'post-Watergate' climate of excessive scrutiny directed against public officials was almost apologetically offered up as an excuse for his fall.

Looking ahead, Gerry Ford was a 'wise nomination.' 'He'll make an excellent vice president,' said Agnew, sounding a pallid echo of Richard Nixon's almost gleeful encomium to Ford on Friday night. As for Agnew, he 'thrived on adversity,' looked forward to the splendid public servants American could pick for President in 1976, and thanked God for the 'opportunity of serving' the American people.

'Thank you, good night and farewell,' he concluded in a tone that, in different circumstances, might be expected to leave no eye dry. Yet, looking at him, one read in the mournful eyes the self-knowledge of a man who expected, at best, a merciful oblivion, a fading away into a never-

never land of embarrassed exile. Yes, a black sheep son in a body politic too polite to allude to him.

He skirted the dollar-and-cents summation of his net worth. The fireworks pre-figured in the Nashville Banner interview, in which he hinted at a Nixon team cabal to destroy him, was also absent. In the end, the man who had acquired a sort of zany stature as a symbol of probity and jugular ferocity lacked the second quality as well as the first. It was as if when the last act came he meekly read the speech the Nixon wordsmiths had shoved in front of him. There was circularity there, for that was how it all began five years ago.

So what was his real net worth? What had he profited from it all? In dollars, a pittance. As a man, he had lost everything and could not even find the words to bluster to explain, or even to apologize.

He faded from the TV, an unfortunate interruption in a fun-filled evening of bogus commercials and mindless entertainment. Before long the nine o'clock ABC Monday Night Football filled the screens. The Cleveland hometown fans waved placards saying 'Spiro Picked Miami' and 'Howard Cosell for vice president.' They were his people, the Silent Majority. They had already grasped that his speech meant nothing, that his net worth stood at zero.

Tom Dowling

Agnew, the truth and a free press

Those who admire Spiro Agnew and the views he espoused so pugnaciously for almost five years are mourning his resignation following his admission of tax evasion in 1967.

Those who have detested the Vice-President and his assaults on 'radical liberals' and 'effete snobs' are openly gleeful, gloating that this glibly sanctimonious advocate of 'law and order' has been exposed as a felon.

But these are not times to continue the polarization of which Agnew once was a red-flag symbol. This is a time for us to deal seriously with the question of how this society can minimize crookedness and criminality in the top levels of government.

We can start by looking at a couple of lessons that leap out from the Agnew tragedy.

Lesson No.1 is that we must start taking closer looks at, and selecting more carefully, the people who spend the public's money, do the public's business and have stewardship over national security.

It must now be apparent that, when great power is there for the taking, very few politicians will voluntarily admit to past indiscretions or crimes which might suggest they are unfit to hold power.

Sen. Thomas Eagleton wanted the Vice-Presidential nomination too much to tell Sen. George McGovern about his medical record. Agnew craved the dubious power of that 'warm bucket of spit' abomination we call the vice Presidency too much to tell president Nixon he had failed to pay taxes on money passed to him in 1967 and that he had taken money from Maryland contractors which some people might consider bribes or payoffs.

The inescapable reality is that no politician with half a brain will ever volunteer anything to suggest that he is less than God's greatest gift to public service. So Lesson No. 2 is this: if the public wants the truth about those who hold power in the country, the people had better ensure that the First Amendment is not eroded and that we always have a free and courageous press.

If that sounds self serving, so be it. The panoply of ugly facts and revelations which have gushed forth into the living rooms and autos and offices of the American people over the last 16 months ought to leave no doubt anywhere that to gag or restrict the press in any way would be to wipe out much of the public's chance to learn of official corruption and malfeasance.

Let us never forget that, even as he lied to the American people with assertions that the charges against him were 'damned lies,' the former Vice-President was seeking to muzzle the press. Agnew tried to portray the press as the vehicle used by an unscrupulous Justice department to convict him unfairly in the court of public opinion.

We now have Agnew's admission of guilt on some of the charges, but during that period when he was criss-crossing the country making pious denials of everything he built up a new wave of public hostility toward the press.

The anti-press campaign went so far that Agnew's lawyers got Judge Walter E. Hoffman to give them unprecedented authority to subpoena newsmen and grill them about the sources of their stories about the Vice-President. They even provoked Hoffman to make some gratuitous remarks about how 'the press is often wrong,' and about what Hoffman perceives to be a war between the press and the courts.

Agnew's resignation and the court proceedings surrounding it show that the press was serving the public's rights to know when it revealed that the No. 2 official in the land was being investigated by top officials from his own party, with suggestions of bribery, extortion, tax evasion and conspiracy.

Not that Judge Hoffman was wrong in saying that the press is often wrong. It is – for the simple reason that news reporters and editors are just like judges. Some are brilliant, some dumb; some compassionate, others vindictive; some balanced in judgment, others psychotic beyond belief; a few humble, most oversupplied with ego.

Before Wednesday's stunning resignation, which made the Hoffman folderol about the press moot, there was real danger that millions of Americans would be misled to believe that the issue at hand was the righteousness of newsmen instead of the innocence and probity of Spiro Agnew.

We were perilously close to a new erosion of the First Amendment because a lot of people much preferred to believe that newsmen are a bunch of bastards rather than even think their Vice-President had failed to pay his taxes.

Democrats and Republicans have been killed politically by enterprising newsmen. So a lot of people of both parties are easily suckered into joining attacks on the First Amendment. But do we need more than Watergate or the Agnew case to convince people to leave alone the constitutional safeguards that have kept this nation great, and reasonably free, for two centuries?

Carl T. Rowan

List of Contributors

Jack Anderson
Donald P. Baker
William F. Buckley Jr.
Lou Cannon
Marquis Childs
Richard M. Cohen
B.D. Colen
Tom Dowling
Rowland Evans
Garnett D. Harner
Peter A. Jay
Norman Kempster
James J. Kilpatrick
Joseph Kraft
Richard L. Lyons

Crosby S. Noyes
Robert Novak
Jerry Oppenheimer
James Reston
William R. Raspberry
Carl T. Rowan
Eileen Shanahan
Ronald Sarro
William Safire
William Taaffe
Tom Wicker
John C. White
Edward Walsh
Joseph Young

and
Associate Press, *United Press International*, the *Star News* and the *Washington Post*